W9-BNU-423

The Official Adobe

Print Publishing Guide

Second Edition

Brian P. Lawler

Adobe

The Official Adobe Print Publishing Guide, Second Edition
Brian P. Lawler

Adobe Press
1249 Eighth Street
Berkeley, CA 94710
510/524-2178
800/283-9444
510/524-2221 (fax)

Find us on the Web at www.adobepress.com.
To report errors, please send a note to errata@peachpit.com.

Adobe Press is an imprint of Peachpit, a division of Pearson Education.

Editor: Rebecca Gulick
Production Editor: Connie Jeung-Mills
Copy Editor: Tiffany Taylor
Proofreader: Alison Kelley
Compositor: Owen Wolfson
Illustrators: Brian P. Lawler and Julie Brockmeyer
Indexer: James Minkin
Cover Design: Charlene Will
Interior Design: Owen Wolfson
Cover and Interior Photography: Brian P. Lawler, Corbis, Getty Images

ISBN 0-321-30466-7

9 8 7 6 5 4

Printed and bound in the United States of America

Thank you to Ellis Myers, who gave me a chance and a lot of education in the graphic arts; to my favorite graphic artist, Ashala; my favorite illustrator, Patrick; all of my instructors and mentors at Cal Poly; Harvey Levenson and Mike Blum, who promised it would be "just one class" they wanted me to teach; to my colleagues Lorraine Donegan, Penny Osmond, Ken Macro, Malcolm Keif, Tom Goglio, Kevin Cooper and Melanie Kronemann; and to Korla McFall, Bob Pinkin and Sabra Scott, staff members par excellence.

—Brian P. Lawler

Contents

CE

Introduction

Until recently, most prepress tasks—such as scanning color photographs, trapping, imposition, color correction, and halftone screening—were performed exclusively by skilled specialists working manually or on expensive proprietary systems. Today many of these tasks can be accomplished on the desktop.

The flexibility and direct control offered by this new technology have blurred the traditional roles of designer and prepress professionals. Designers who have the knowledge and the equipment can do their own prepress work. The prepress industry has changed to support the new requirements of the desktop publisher. Most commercial print shops are now equipped to image a file directly onto lithographic plates without requiring film as an intermediary, or even directly from a digital file to press.

Managing these changing relationships to achieve output of professional quality requires a knowledge of the processes and relevant issues. As a guide to the preparation of electronic files for commercial printing, this book addresses these issues and supplies the information you will need in deciding whether to perform a particular task yourself or to leave that task in the hands of a prepress professional.

1 Color and Commercial Printing

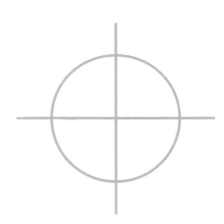

Color and Commercial Printing

One of the greatest challenges designers and publishers face is ensuring that the color in their printed artwork looks the way they intend. Accurate color reproduction requires a solid understanding of color basics and how color is displayed and printed on different devices, as well as good communication between the designer, the prepress provider, and the commercial printer.

This chapter introduces fundamental printing concepts and terminology and describes several processes that are commonly used to produce commercial printing.

Describing Color

Objects appear to be certain colors because of their ability to reflect, absorb, or transmit light; we perceive this light as color. Our eyes are sensitive enough to perceive a nearly infinite range of colors in the spectrum of visible light—including many colors that can't be displayed on a computer screen or printed on a commercial printing press.

We describe color in terms of three characteristics: hue, saturation, and brightness. These qualities are traditionally represented graphically on a *color wheel. Brightness* has to do with the quantity of light reaching your eye—the brightness of a surface depends on how reflective it is. *Hues* depend on wavelength and are identified by color names; a hue corresponds to a direction on the color wheel. *Saturation*, sometimes called *chroma,* refers to a color's vividness.

Two colors have the same hue and brightness but differ in saturation if one appears whiter or more neutral. Spectral colors—the colors of a single wavelength of light from a prism—have maximum saturation. The saturation of a pure spectral color can be reduced while keeping the brightness steady by diluting the color with white light. On a color wheel, which has spectral colors along the rim, white at the center, and uniform brightness, saturation corresponds to distance from the center of the wheel.

Each type of device used to create a color publication—be it a scanner, computer display, color desktop printer, or commercial printing press—reproduces a different range of color, or color *gamut*. Even similar devices, such as two computer displays made by the same manufacturer, can show the same color differently. You can view more vivid colors on your display than you can print on a desktop printer or a commercial printing press. Special inks can also create printed colors that can't be represented on a computer display. In addition, scanners, digital cameras and computer displays use different models to describe color from those used by desktop printers and commercial presses. As colors move from the computer display to the printing press, they're converted from one color environment to another, resulting in sometimes-dramatic changes.

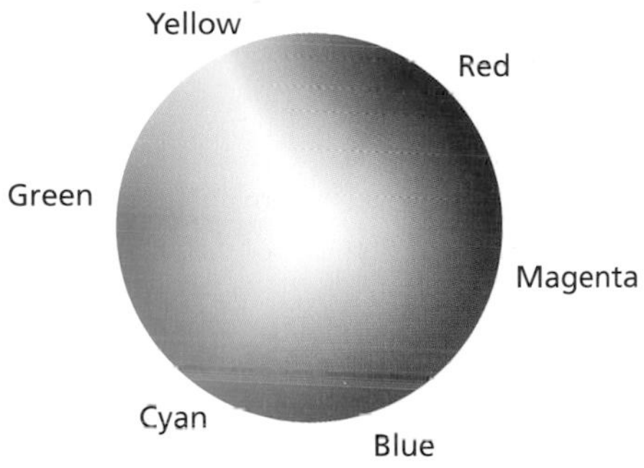

Color Wheel

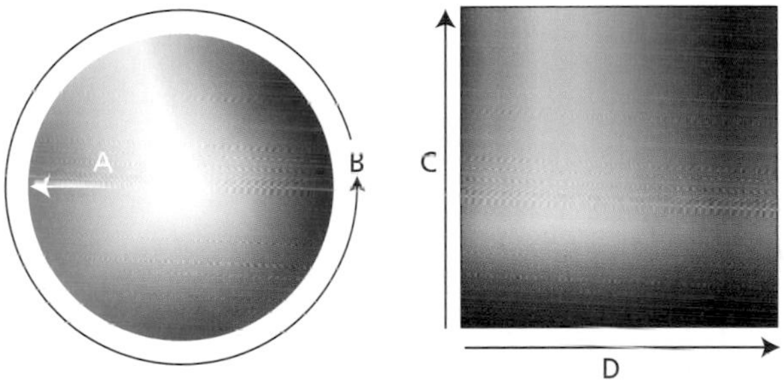

A. Saturation B. Hue C. Brightness D. All hues

Color models

Designers can use different models to select and manipulate color, corresponding to the way color is generated in different media. On a television screen or computer display, a spot on the screen *emits* varying amounts of red, green, and blue (RGB) light that combine to define the spot's color. When you manipulate color (using an image-editing program, for example), you have the option of working in the RGB model and specifying colors by their red, green, and blue components.

The color printing process uses four transparent inks: cyan, magenta, yellow (CMY), and black (K). The black is used to define detail in images, to deepen shadows, and to print type and graphics in black. When you define color using computer software, you have the option of working in either the RGB or the CMYK mode, and you may decide to convert images from one color space to the other.

Red, green, and blue are the *additive primaries* of light. If you combine 100 percent of red, green, and blue *light,* you see white. If none of the additive primaries are present, you perceive black. When discussing printing inks, cyan, magenta, and yellow *pigments* are the *subtractive primaries.* They *filter* components of red, green, and blue from white light, and you see what remains. For example, if a printed sample absorbs all the red light striking it and reflects the green and blue, its color is cyan.

If you combine 100 percent of cyan, magenta, and yellow ink on paper, the result is complete absorption, or black—in theory. Impurities in printing ink pigments cause the combination of cyan, magenta, and yellow to create a color that is *not quite black;* black ink is added to compensate for that.

Some computer applications, like Adobe Illustrator, require that the entire document be in one color space—RGB or CMYK. When you create a new document in Illustrator, you must select one of the two. After an Illustrator document is created, you can switch it to the other color system by changing the Document Color Mode under the File menu. *Spot colors,* like those defined with the Pantone color system, can be used in either document color environment.

Image-editing programs such as Adobe Photoshop require an image to be in one of several color spaces (typically RGB or CMYK) but provide several color selection options besides RGB and CMYK. These include the hue, saturation, brightness (HSB) palette, which lets you choose colors by the color wheel method; and the Lab color model, which uses the coordinates of colorimetry. When you're working in Photoshop, you can select a color using any of its palettes even though the document exists in the RGB or CMYK color space.

Adobe InDesign documents readily accept color images in a variety of color spaces (typically RGB, monochrome, or CMYK) without requiring any conversion. InDesign shares the Color Settings of Adobe Photoshop; when you open a document, it adopts the default color settings it finds in Color Settings.

Additive color model: RGB

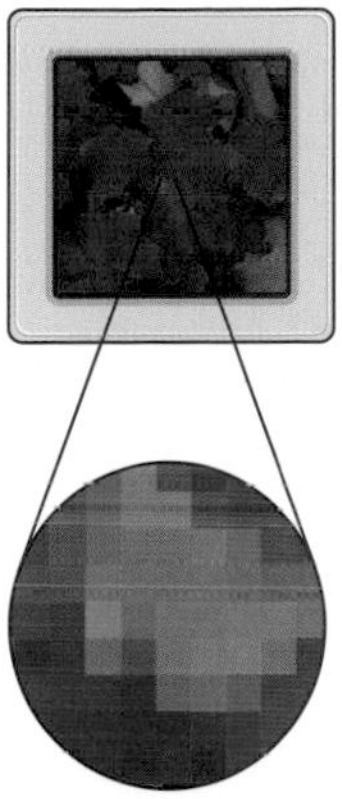

Monitor pixels

The three additive primaries of light are red, green, and blue. When combined in pairs, they make cyan, magenta and yellow. When all three are combined, you see white. Computer displays emit light in additive colors, displaying it as pixels on the screen.

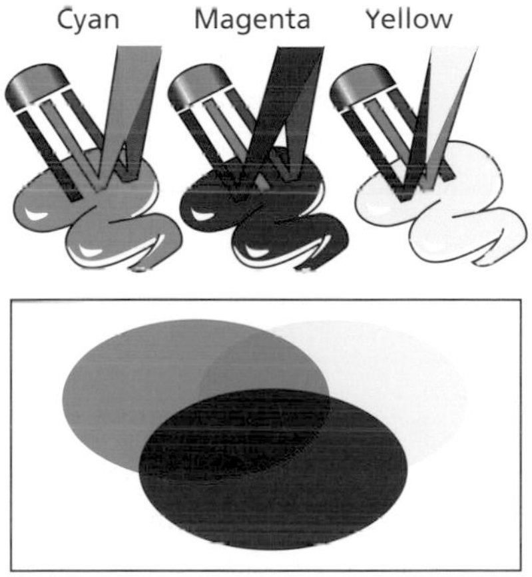

Subtractive color model: CMY

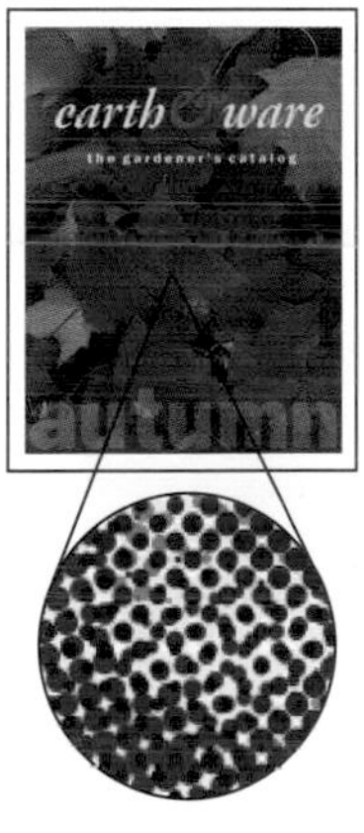

Printed dots

When working with printer's ink, the subtractive color primaries are used—cyan, magenta, and yellow. They are called subtractive because they act as filters, subtracting color from white light. When mixed in pairs, they make red, green, and blue. When combined, they make a muddy brown color, a result of slight impurities in the pigments used to make ink. To get a good black, printing processes add black ink to supplement the cyan, magenta, and yellow primary colors, thus CMYK process color.

Color gamuts

The range of colors a device can reproduce, capture or display is called its color *gamut*. The gamut of most output devices, including printers, is a fraction of the visible color spectrum. The color gamuts of different devices typically overlap but don't coincide; these differences often result in the same color appearing different in different contexts. To help guarantee consistent color across output devices, computer applications use color management systems. These systems embed files with color profiles to ensure consistent color through all stages of production.

By having a description of each device's color gamut in the workflow, a program that performs color management can coordinate color reproduction at each stage of a print project—scanning, design, proofing, and print—and help the designer achieve acceptable and predictable color in the final copy.

CIE xyY color space

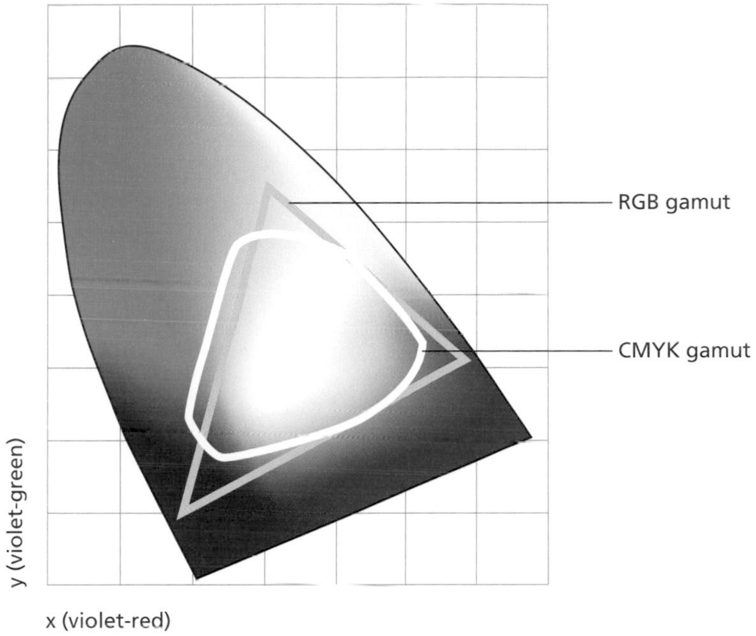

Color management with ICC profiles

The *ICC profile* is a standardized software component developed by the International Color Consortium for describing the color behavior of any device. These profiles can be embedded in images and used to process colors when scanning, viewing, and printing. Profiles provide a description of the color behavior of each device in the workflow so that each application performing color management can reliably manage color precision at each stage of a print project.

Adobe added ICC color management as a foundation technology in Photoshop beginning with version 5.0. Today, nearly every image that is processed through Photoshop contains an identifying embedded ICC profile (Photoshop calls this the *Color Working Space*). These embedded ICC profiles provide information about colors as they were captured by the digital camera or scanner and make possible reliable color reproduction without guesswork.

When you're working with programs like Adobe InDesign, color management lets you create page-layout documents that use images *in their original color space*; these images can then be printed by one or more printing processes without converting the original images. For example, you can place photos in RGB color, CMYK color, or grayscale in a page layout, and then print them to CMYK, Hexachrome, monochrome, or another destination color environment without needing to convert the original images. The processing of the color occurs at print time, guided by the embedded profiles and the color-management software running on the computer printing the document.

Using this method, a single document can be printed both on glossy paper on a sheet-fed press and to newsprint on a roll-fed press without modifying the original document images. The color characteristics of the output are optimized for the printing process, paper, and ink according to the *output profile* that defines how the color is converted for the specific printing process.

For more information on color management, see "Using a Color Management System" on page 60.

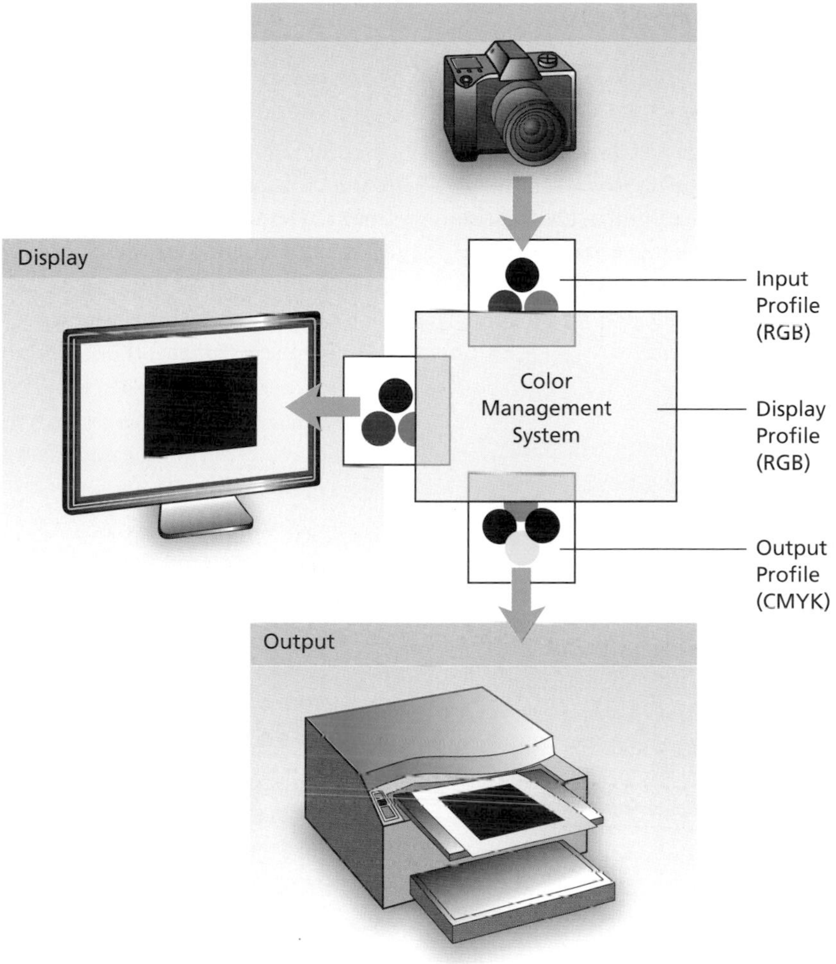
Display
Input
Profile
(RGB)
Color
Management
System
Display
Profile
(RGB)
Output
Profile
(CMYK)
Output

Prepress Terms

Blueline

A diazo (UV-exposed and self-processed) photo print made to proof pagination, image position, and type. Bluelines have been made mostly obsolete by the digital revolution.

Camera-ready

Said of text or artwork ready to be photographed by a process camera.

DPI

An abbreviation for *dots per inch.* Refers to the resolution at which a device, such as a monitor or printer, can display text and graphics.

Continuous-tone art and line art

Continuous-tone art is art, such as photographs, that consists of shades of gray and color gradations. It's distinguished from line art, such as a line drawing, which has no tonal variation. If you look closely at continuous-tone art, you can see that shades of gray or color blend smoothly without breaking into dots or other patterns. When the art is printed, the corresponding regions are reproduced as arrays of different-sized dots printed in the colors used on the press.

Dot gain

Many variables—from ink to paper surface and press used—affect the size of halftone dots. A certain amount of *dot gain*, or increase in halftone dot size, occurs naturally when wet ink spreads as it's absorbed by the paper. If too much dot gain occurs, images and colors print darker than specified.

Dot gain is one of the characteristics taken into account when color-management systems are applied.

(See page 110 for more information on dot gain.)

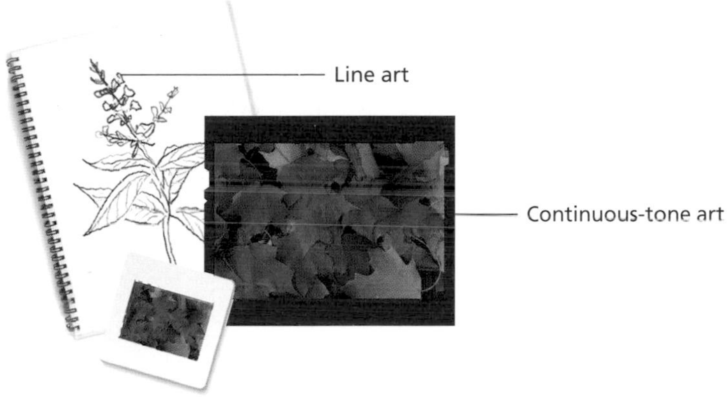

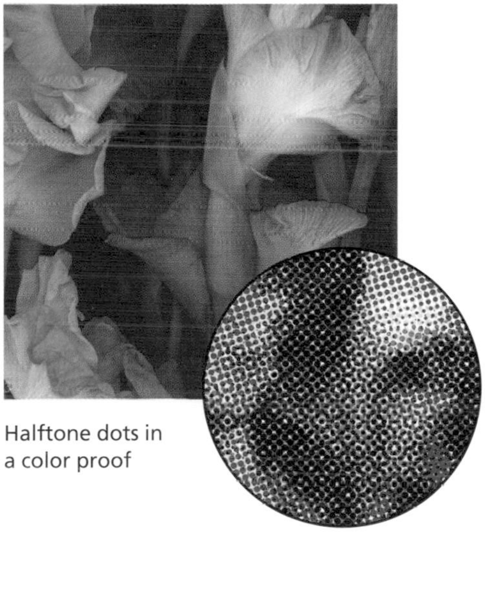

Halftone dots in
a color proof

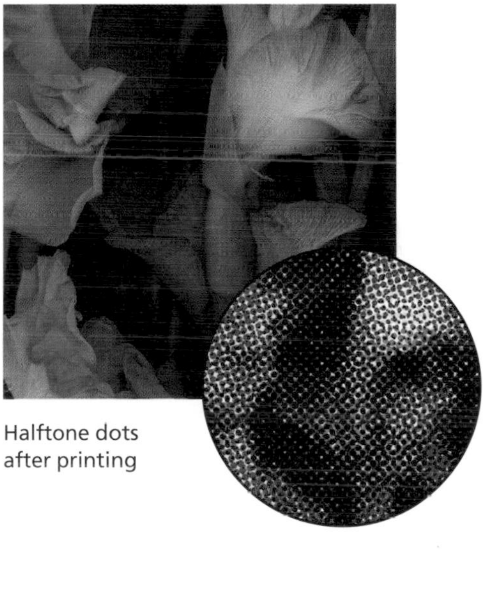

Halftone dots
after printing

Halftone screens

Ink is an all-or-nothing medium in the sense that any spot on the paper is either inked full-strength or not at all. To simulate shades of gray or color on a commercial press, the image must be broken into arrays of dots of various sizes using *halftone screening.*

In the case of black-and-white photography, black dots are used to simulate shades of gray. Areas where the dots are small appear light gray, and areas where the dots are large appear dark gray or black. The human eye is tricked into seeing tonality by its ability to average the tiny printed dots into the background paper. You "see" gray when you're really looking at small printed black dots on a field of white paper.

To achieve a satisfactory range of color, the printing press superimposes four arrays of dots—in cyan, magenta, yellow, and black ink. A region with larger dots appears darker than a region with smaller dots. The positioning, or *register,* of the four arrays on top of each other is critical to quality printing.

Any visible pattern of interference between the four arrays is distracting. To minimize the chance of interference, each array is oriented at a different angle on the press.

Image resolution (ppi)

Image resolution is the number of pixels displayed per unit of length in an image, usually measured in *pixels per inch.* An image with a high resolution contains more, and therefore smaller, pixels than an image of the same dimensions with a low resolution. For best results, use an image resolution that is greater than the printer's resolution (a factor of 2x is appropriate).

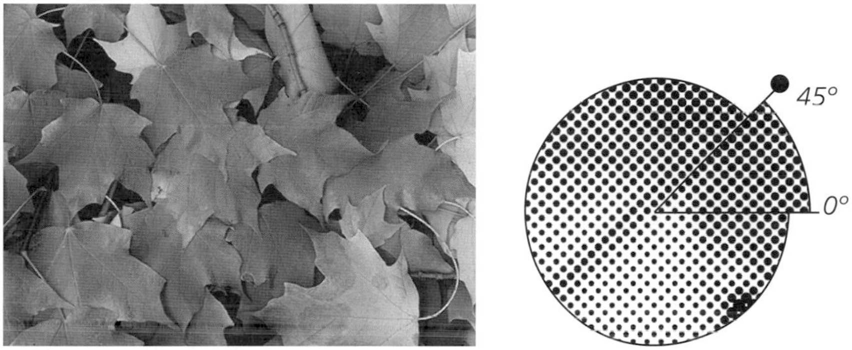

Halftone screen with black ink

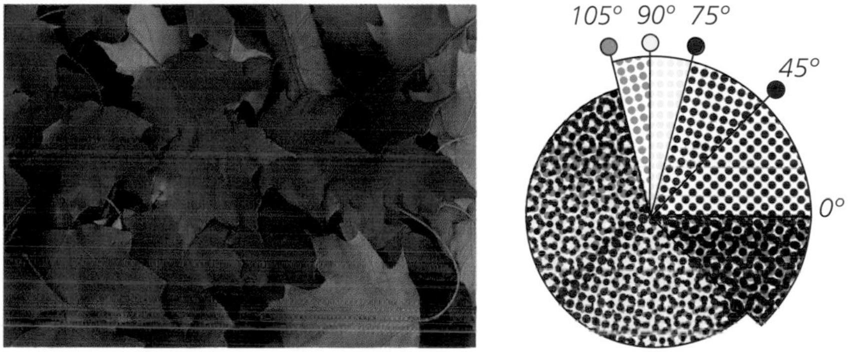

Halftone screens with process inks at different screen angles; correctly registered halftone dots form rosette patterns.

Knocking out and overprinting

When artwork involves two objects or colored regions that overlap each other, a designer can choose either to let the top object eliminate, or *knock out,* what is beneath it or to allow *overprinting.*

In most cases, you want an object to knock out the one below it, to avoid unintended color blends. However, you can use overprinting to create special effects or to hide errors in press register (see "Trapping" on page 24).

Adobe Illustrator and InDesign both feature an Overprint Preview menu selection that can help you see the effect of overprinting colors.

Line screen (lpi)

Line screen, also called *screen ruling* or *screen frequency*, is the number of halftone dots per linear inch used to print grayscale or color images. Line screen is measured in lines per inch (lpi)—or lines of cells per inch in a halftone screen. It gets its name from acid-etched lines on glass screens that were originally used in graphic arts cameras to divide an image into microscopic *circles of confusion*—which, by varying exposure, create halftone dots. The electronic evolution of the halftone uses a *virtual screen* to create its halftone dots.

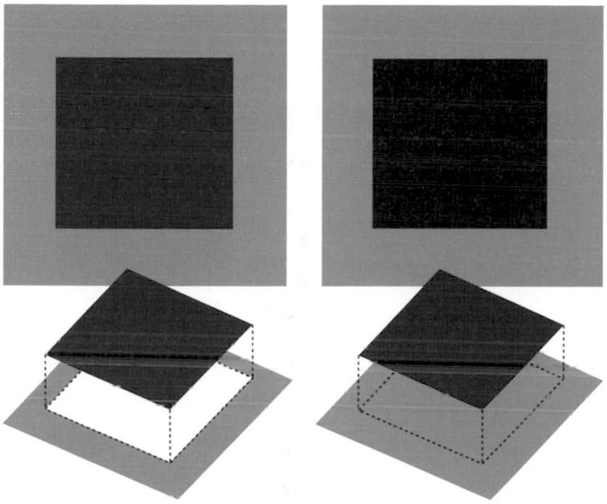

Knockout

Overprint

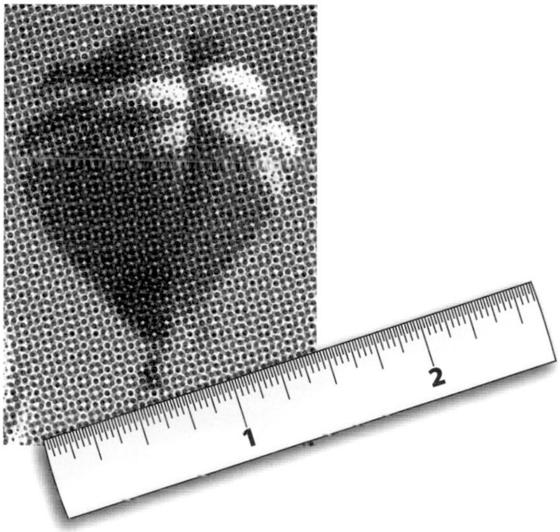

Machine resolution

Output devices like film imagesetters and platesetters have extraordinarily high resolution. Their minimum imageable mark is called a *device pixel* (sometimes called a *machine spot*). A 300-dpi laser printer uses a 1/300" square device pixel; a 600-dpi printer uses a 1/600" square device pixel. Film imagesetters, which are capable of much higher resolutions, can make a mark as small as a 1/3600" square dot. Modern platesetters have resolutions as great as 1/5000". By comparison, most computer displays work with device pixels that are 1/72" square—quite coarse, compared to printing processes.

Misregister

Paper sometimes stretches and shifts as it absorbs moisture and is pulled through a press. Printing plates can also be mounted out of alignment. These factors can cause multicolor jobs to print out of register, resulting in slight gaps or hue shifts between adjacent colors. Trapping and overprinting can conceal some of these flaws. Misregister can also cause images to appear blurred or out of focus. If a press has printed out of register enough to cause images to appear unsightly, the press run should be made again with colors in register.

Moiré patterns

When process-color separations are printed, the arrays of dots for each color are oriented at different angles to minimize interference patterns. The screens are positioned so that the dots form a symmetrical pattern called a *rosette,* which the human eye merges into continuous-tone color.

The relationship between the screen angles is critical. Occasionally, a pattern in a photo (woven furniture and herringbone fabrics are common culprits) interferes with one or more screen angles, causing a noticeable pattern of interference lines called a *moiré pattern.* These patterns are also caused by attempting to print photos that have been scanned from already-printed material. Moiré patterns from printed sheets can be removed by some scanner software and also by techniques in Adobe Photoshop. It isn't advisable to scan printed material, because the result will almost certainly produce a moiré pattern.

When moiré patterns show up in normal printing processes, it can be an indication of a problem in the prepress or platesetting software.

In register

Out of register

PDF (Portable Document Format)

PDF is a document format developed by Adobe for handling documents in a device- and platform-independent manner. It allows files to be viewed, transmitted, printed, and archived in a single format. The PDF format works on all major operating systems, including Mac OS, Windows, and Unix. Adobe Acrobat software provides for the conversion of documents into PDF and allows documents to be created from any application on any computer platform. When converted into PDF, documents can retain a full range of color, graphics, and high-quality typography. Reduced-resolution PDF files make it possible to transfer them efficiently over the Internet for copy checking and on-screen proofing.

Process colors

In the four-color printing process, color is reproduced using transparent pigments of cyan, magenta, and yellow (CMY). These are called *process colors.* In theory, process colors create shades of gray when combined in equal combination and black when combined at full strength. Because of impurities in the inks, however, equal amounts of the three don't produce neutral gray, and full-strength inks combine to create a muddy brown. To achieve contrast and detail in shadows, and to assist in maintaining neutral grays, black ink (also transparent, and identified by the letter K) is added to the three process colors.

Using black ink to replace neutral combinations of C, M, and Y is also economical for printing and helps to maintain the neutrality of midtones.

PostScript

The PostScript language is a page description language developed by Adobe as a way to describe to a printer the image on a page. The introduction of PostScript printers created the electronic publishing revolution. PostScript has become the standard way for a computer to communicate with a printer, imagesetter, or platesetter.

RIP (Raster Image Processor)

The RIP interprets the PostScript code sent from a computer application and then translates that code into instructions for the marking engine that marks the pixels on the paper, film, or plate. A RIP is built into all PostScript desktop printers and is a separate component for imagesetters and platesetters. Some RIPs are software based.

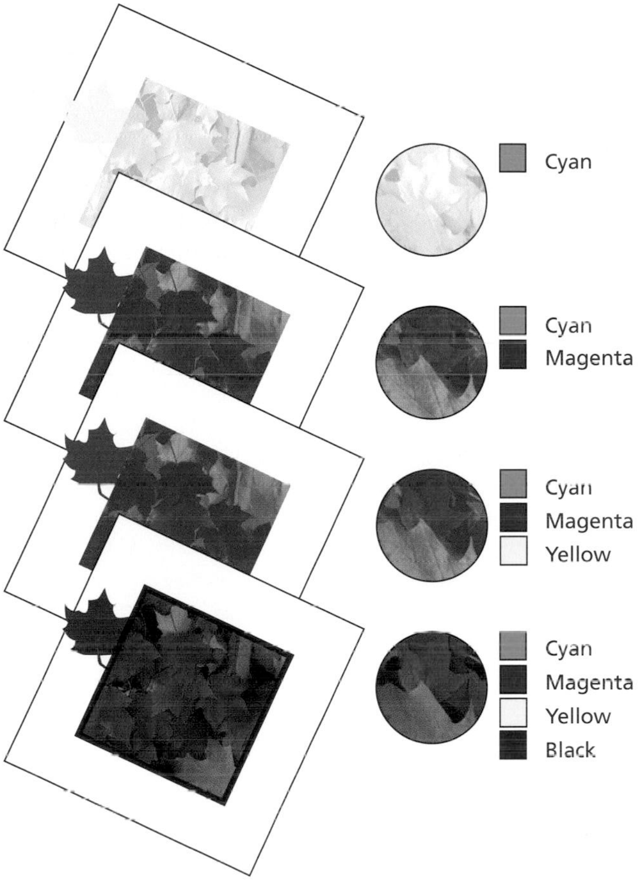
Cyan
Cyan
Magenta
Cyan
Magenta
Yellow
Cyan
Magenta
Yellow
Black

Separations

To print color artwork and images on a commercial press, each page is separated into component images called *color separations*. Traditionally, separations were created photographically through colored filters, with the results exposed onto large sheets of film. Today, separations are created digitally. There are usually four separations per page, one for each of the CMYK process colors and one for each spot color being used.

Within each separation, photographs are screened into an array of halftone dots (or similar patterns). Type, line-art illustrations, and similar graphics are either printed as solids of colors or screened into halftone patterns according to the assigned values in the originating document.

Designers generally don't produce separations; instead, they provide complete digital files to the printer for production. In modern printing, the separation of colors in a printed document is done as part of platesetting.

Spot colors and tints

Spot color refers to color printed using inks *other* than process colors. Each spot color is produced using a single ink and printing plate. You can choose from among hundreds of different spot-color inks.

Spot color may be used to reproduce colors not within the CMYK gamut. A spot color may also be used to *bump*, or boost, the density of a process color. Spot color is often used to save money when only one or two colors are needed—a job can then be printed on a less-expensive two-color printing press. (See page 54 for guidelines on choosing spot colors.)

A spot color printed at 100 percent density is a solid color and has no dot pattern. A *tint* is a lightened spot or process color created by printing that ink with halftone dots. This process is typically referred to as *screening*.

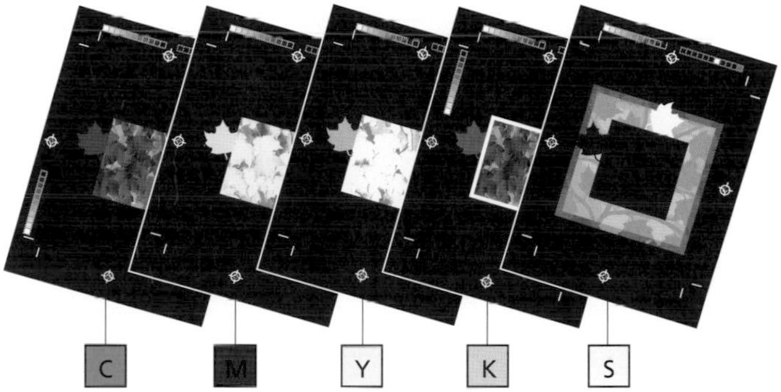
C
M
Y
K
S

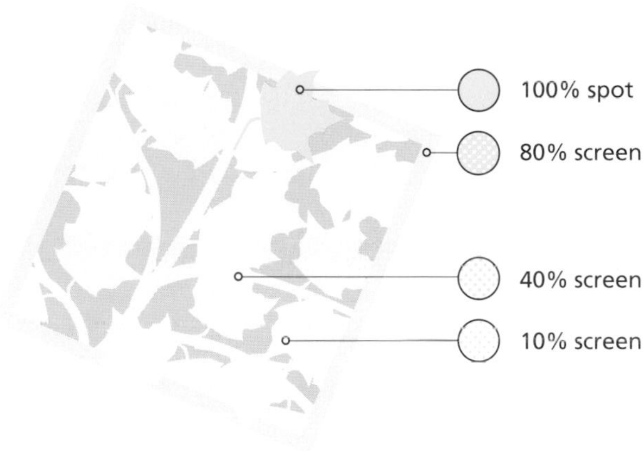
100% spot
80% screen
40% screen
10% screen

Trapping

The quality of a printer's work depends on getting the different inks to print *in register*—that is, exactly aligned with each other. If one or more inks print out of register, white gaps may appear between adjacent objects where the paper shows through, and there may be fringes of unexpected color. To minimize the effects of misregister, commercial printers use a technique called *color trapping*: adjacent colors are *intentionally* set to overprint along common boundaries. Trapping can be done manually in an illustration or an image-editing program, but today much of it is done by sophisticated processes in prepress production software.

Undercolor removal (UCR) and gray-component replacement (GCR)

At any point on the page where the three CMY inks are used at combined percentages to produce gray, the combination can be replaced by black. To avoid having too much ink on the page (which can cause drying problems), printers use techniques called *undercolor removal* (UCR) and *gray-component replacement* (GCR). With UCR, cyan, magenta, and yellow colors are reduced slightly to put the right amount of ink on the page and thereby allow the ink to dry. With GCR, black ink replaces much of the cyan, magenta, and yellow in neutral gray areas according to a complex formula.

Printing with GCR separations allows neutral colors to be printed with better color consistency. This is particularly beneficial on high-speed web-fed printing presses and for screen printing, where maintaining gray balance can be challenging. Sheet-fed printing is more commonly done with UCR separations, because the presses run more slowly and neutral balance is easier to control.

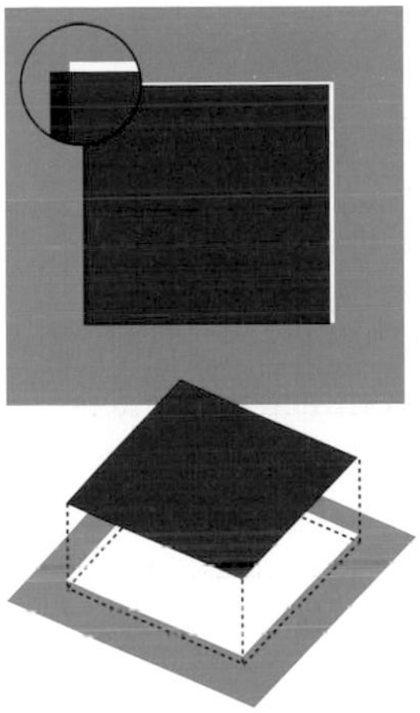

Misregister with no trap

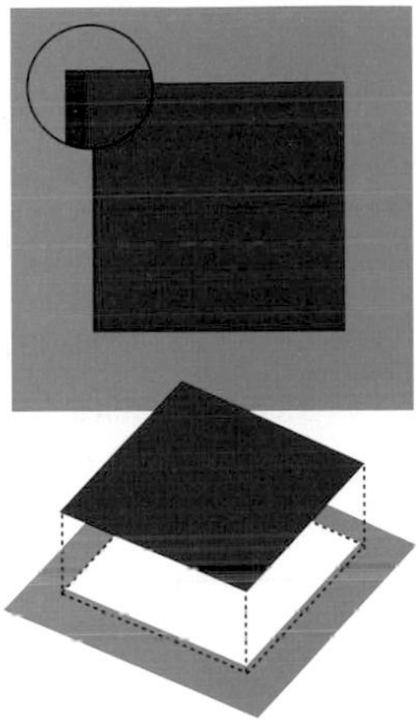

Misregister with trap

UCR

UCR CMY

UCR Black

GCR 50%

GCR 50% CMY

GCR 50% Black

GCR 100%

GCR 100% CMY

GCR 100% Black

Computer Graphics

Vector graphics

Vector graphics are created in illustration programs like Adobe Illustrator. The objects in vector graphics are made up of mathematically defined curve and line segments. You can edit such a graphic by moving and resizing the entire graphic or selected components. Curves in vector graphics are determined by the points you select for the lines to pass through; you change the shape of a curve by dragging its control points.

Because the objects that form them are defined mathematically, vector graphics take up comparatively little space and aren't tied to a particular resolution. When displayed or printed, the graphics are calculated to fit whatever screen or printer is used. Vector graphics are therefore considered *resolution-independent* and *scaleable*. Unlike raster images (described next), they can be output to different-sized screens or printing technologies of varying resolution at any size without any quality loss.

Photos placed in vector illustrations don't share their independence of resolution. Too much enlargement of an illustration containing a placed photo will reveal visible pixels.

Raster images

Digital photographs are *raster images,* also called *bitmap images.* They exist in a rectangular grid of small squares called *pixels.* Each pixel contains data that describes its gray level or color value. Raster images take up more space on disk than vector graphics do, often tens or hundreds of megabytes.

Because a raster image is made up of a fixed number of pixels, the dimensions at which the image is output depend on its resolution. A square raster that is 100 pixels wide, for example, will have a resolution of 100 pixels per inch if printed in an inch-wide square. If printed at twice the size, however, it will have half the resolution *in both dimensions* and thus one-quarter the overall resolution.

Unlike vector graphics, which are edited by altering mathematical lines and shapes, raster images are edited by manipulating groups of pixels. Because a raster image inhabits a grid, problems can be associated with enlarging it or moving it to a grid with more available pixels. In a simple enlargement, the individual pixels are enlarged and may become visible as jagged lines. In transferring an image to a grid with more pixels, the colors or gray levels for the new pixels must be inferred by a process of interpolation that may cause blurring.

Vector graphics describe
shapes mathematically.

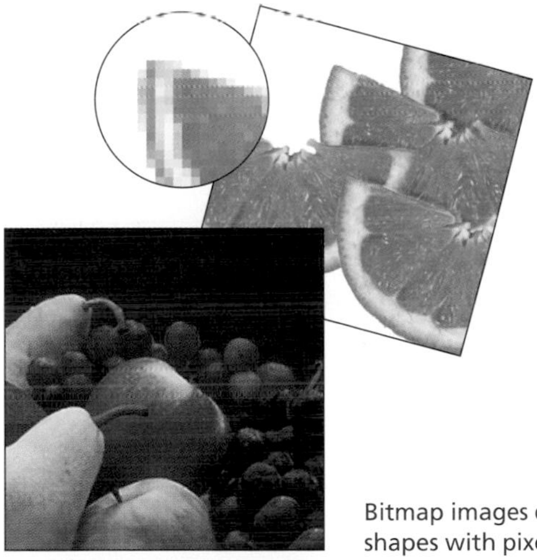

Bitmap images describe
shapes with pixels.

Image Resolution and Line Screen

Spatial resolution, typically some number of dots per inch, corresponds roughly to the ability to render graphic detail. On a computer screen, it's the number of pixels per linear inch (ppi); on an output device, it's the number of dots printed in a linear inch (dpi); on a scanner, it's the number of pixels sampled per linear inch of the scanned image. The resolution of a raster image depends on the size it's printed as well as on the pixel dimensions of the file. Pixel dimensions determine file s tical matter, file size is related to storage and processing efficiencies.

If you're scanning images from film or prints, you have control over the resolution, and you can choose whatever value you think will produce the best results. If the resolution is unnecessarily high, files will take a long time to display and print; if the resolution is too low, the quality of output will suffer. The choice of resolution should be based on the intended printing process—which usually defines the halftone screen frequency—and the subject matter of the image.

As a general rule, the scan resolution should be double the lines per inch (lpi) you intend to use for halftone screening, although this can vary. With naturally textured images, such as images of water and foliage and many portraits, you may get good results with an image resolution that is one-and-a-half times the screen frequency.

You can also use lower resolutions with nontraditional forms of screening, such as *stochastic* (frequency-modulated) screening. Use high resolution where detail is critical and where lines must be sharp, as with images of electronic products, jewelry, and machinery. Because resolution and reproduction size balance each other, accepting less than the traditional 2:1 resolution ratio means that an image can be reproduced at a slightly larger size.

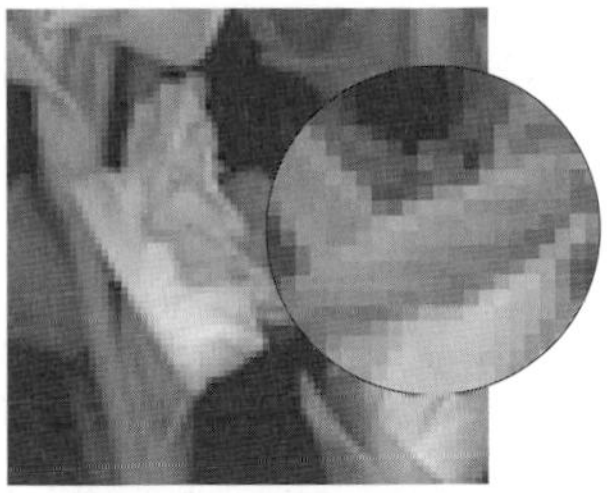

Image resolution: 72 ppi

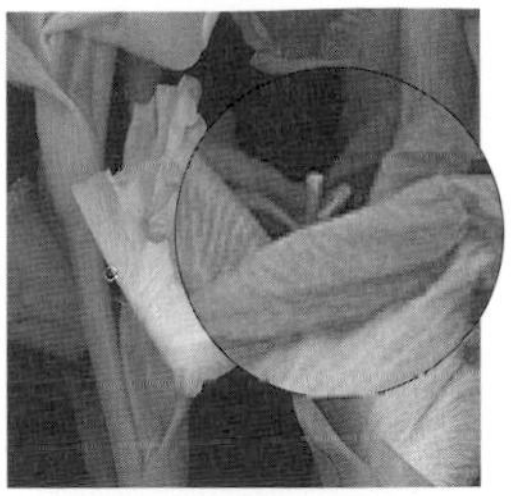

Image resolution: 300 ppi

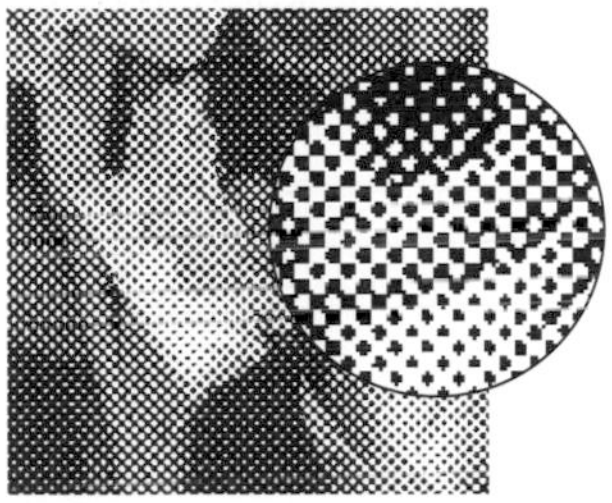

Image resolution: 300 ppi
Output resolution: 300 dpi

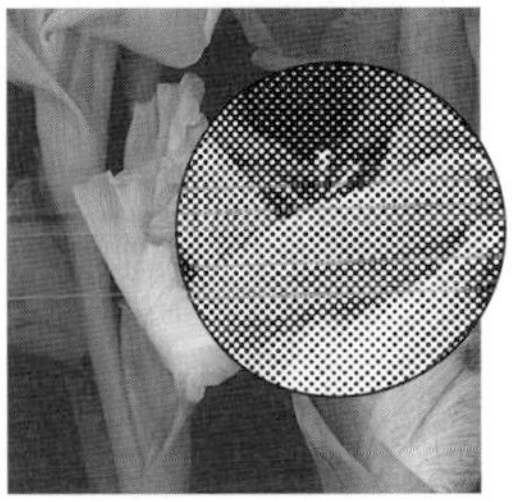

Image resolution: 300 ppi
Output resolution: 2400 dpi

65 lpi: Coarse screen used for screen printing

133 lpi: Fine screen often used for magazines

85 lpi: Average screen often used for newspapers

150 lpi: Fine screen often used for commercial printing

Printing Technologies

Frequency-modulated and hybrid screening

Traditional halftone screening arranges image dots of varying size into a regular grid pattern. Frequency-modulated (FM) screening (also called *stochastic screening*) arranges dots in irregular clumps rather than in an orderly formation. Screens made this way don't have repeating beats and are generally free from moiré patterns. To use FM screening, you need special software or a platesetter that supports the process.

Traditional halftone screening uses the size of the dot to modulate between gray levels: larger dots for darker shades, smaller dots for lighter shades. Frequency-modulated screening controls the level of gray or color by varying the composition of clumps and how close the clumps are to each other. It distributes dots semi-randomly but still controls the number of dots in each space: more dots produce a darker effect, fewer dots produce a lighter effect.

In addition to its freedom from moiré patterns, FM screening has another advantage over traditional halftones. Because it uses mostly small dots to make its impression, images usually display more detail in the highlights. On the other end of the tonal scale, colors that should be solid may appear grainy. Stochastic screening also has measurably greater dot gain than an equivalent conventional halftone process, which requires strict control in the platesetting process.

Recent advances in stochastic screening have delivered *hybrid screening* processes that put FM patterns in the highlights while using conventional halftone dots in the shadows.

High-fidelity color printing

Much research has gone into expanding the range of colors produced by process color printing. One of the solutions is to print additional inks, such as red, green, and blue; or green and orange. The addition of these inks produces a much larger color gamut but poses challenges to the traditional color separation process (and requires a printing press with more than four units). Stochastic screening plays an important role in the success of high-fidelity color printing because it allows additional inks to be printed without risk of duplicate screen angles and moiré patterns.

Pantone Hexachrome is a commercial high-fidelity color system supported by Photoshop, InDesign, and QuarkXPress. This system enables printing with six process inks (CMYK plus orange and green) to produce a greater gamut of colors on press. Six-color printing presses are common today, making Hexachrome and other high-fidelity printing more practical.

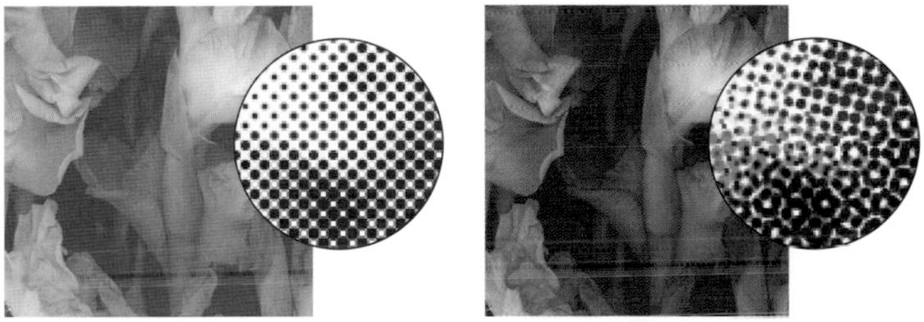

Conventional halftone screening

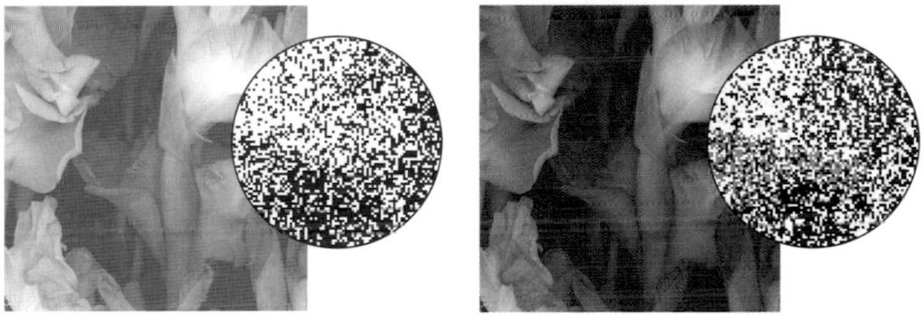

FM screening

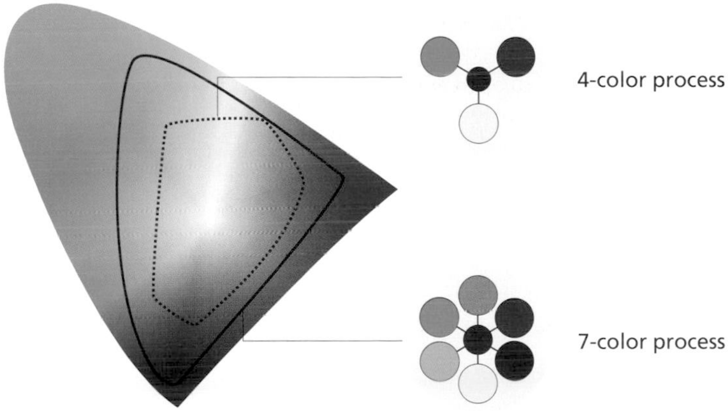

Imagesetters

An *imagesetter* is a device for marking photographic film with the data necessary for printing. These machines use lasers to expose rolls of graphic arts film to produce either positive or negative images that are later exposed to an aluminum printing plate for printing. Driven by a Raster Image Processor (RIP), imagesetters produce very high resolution text, graphics, and images to film.

A generation of newer platesetters has replaced most imagesetters in the printing industry, but film imagesetters are still used in the screen printing and flexographic printing fields where film sheets are a necessity of image processing.

Direct-digital printing presses

In direct-digital printing, presses are networked to workstations that create PostScript files from digital documents, process document components, and send the files to the press. The presses don't require film or, in some cases, printing plates. Some direct-digital presses transfer digital information onto electrophotographic cylinders instead of plates and use toner to print four-color pages. Other presses expose the digitized pages directly to special plates mounted on the press.

Direct-digital printing produces fast turnaround times, low production costs, and the ability to personalize publications. Digital printing is often used for variable-data printing, on-demand printing, or short-run color printing, where a small number of copies are printed. It isn't suited for high-volume print jobs.

Variable-data printing

Digital presses create the opportunity for a new kind of printed marketing using presses that can change the copy and images for every impression they print. Called *Variable-Data Printing* (VDP), these documents can have varying text, personalized graphics, photos that change according the demographic information of the recipient, and more.

VDP is created with a combination of page-layout applications, database records, libraries of variable images, and special software that defines which components go together for each recipient.

VDP products have been shown to improve the response to printed marketing efforts. They're compelling because they bring individualized printing out of the category of junk mail and into the category of one-to-one marketing. When created with properly filtered data, these individualized marketing pieces are often read with more interest by their recipients, and response rates are measurably better.

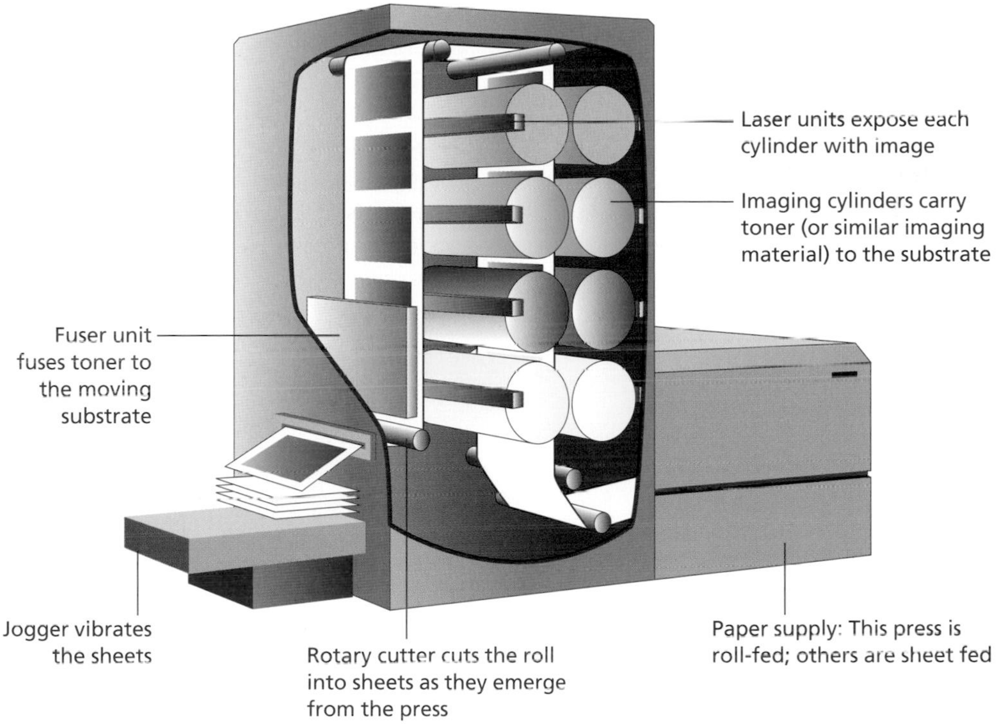
Laser units expose each cylinder with image
Imaging cylinders carry toner (or similar imaging material) to the substrate
Fuser unit fuses toner to the moving substrate
Jogger vibrates the sheets
Rotary cutter cuts the roll into sheets as they emerge from the press
Paper supply: This press is roll-fed; others are sheet fed

Computer-to-plate systems

Computer-to-plate (CTP) devices work like film imagesetters, but they expose an image directly onto an aluminum or polyester surface rather than a piece of film. This eliminates a costly and time-consuming step on the way to press. CTP produces higher print quality by avoiding generations of film processing and exposure, and it features higher resolution than its film counterparts.

CTP devices accept PostScript files and can produce images with either conventional screening or stochastic pattern imaging. Platesetters also reduce the printing industry's dependence on photo chemistry and produce output with no environmentally dangerous waste byproducts.

The plate is held to the internal drum by vacuum

Plates are hand-fed into this machine.
Some platesetters have auto-feed

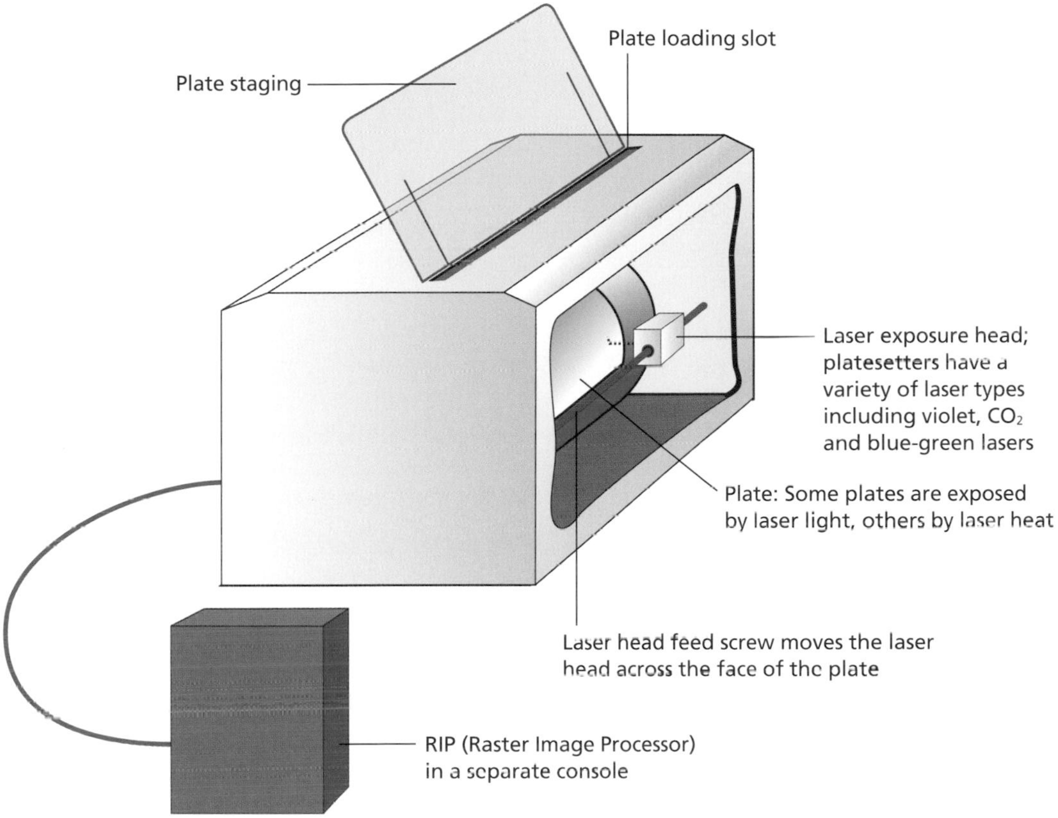

Offset Lithography

You can choose from several different processes to print a publication: flexography, intaglio (gravure), screen printing, and offset lithography are the most common. The method you choose depends on your budget, your choice of a commercial printer, and the printed results you want. Because offset lithography is the most common printing process, we use it here to explain the basics of commercial printing.

Offset lithography involves printing from a flat printing surface. The printing plate holds ink because the image area is treated to make it chemically receptive to oil-based ink but not to water—not because the image area is raised (as in flexography) or etched (as in gravure).

A multicolor offset press has a separate printing unit for each ink being printed. For example, if you're using process colors and one spot color in a print job and your commercial printer's press can handle five inks, a printing unit will be set up for each ink. The paper will then pass through each unit in succession. If the press handles fewer inks, your printer will print two or three inks first, stop the press and change the inks, and then run the paper through again to print the remaining inks.

Platemaking Using a laser or photographic process, a printer exposes the document onto a flat plate with a smooth coating and then processes the plate to remove the nonimages areas. Nonimage areas are porous aluminum, which is attractive to water.

Dampening The plate is mounted on a cylinder. When the press starts, the plate comes into contact with dampener rollers first. Dampening solution (water plus additives) flows constantly from a fountain through a series of rollers to the plate cylinder. The last roller dampens the entire printing plate.

Inking Next, the ink roller applies oil-based ink to the plate. Thick ink flows from another fountain through a series of rollers, which distribute the ink thinly and evenly. When the last ink roller contacts the dampened printing plate, it smoothly distributes the ink across the water-resistant image area. The adjustment of ink and water must be balanced before printing can be done.

Printing The unique roller in an offset press is the *blanket cylinder,* which carries away a reversed image from the plate and transfers this image to the paper. The blanket has some resiliency and gives slightly when pressed against paper, so the image can transfer evenly to smooth or textured papers. The blanket is also formulated to accept ink but reject the dampener solution, leaving most of the water behind.

In the printing step, the paper—in individual sheets—passes between the blanket cylinder and the impression cylinder. The blanket cylinder carries the ink from the plate, presses against the paper, and transfers the ink onto the paper. On web-fed offset presses, two blanket cylinders belonging to two press units print both sides of the roll simultaneously, so there is no impression cylinder.

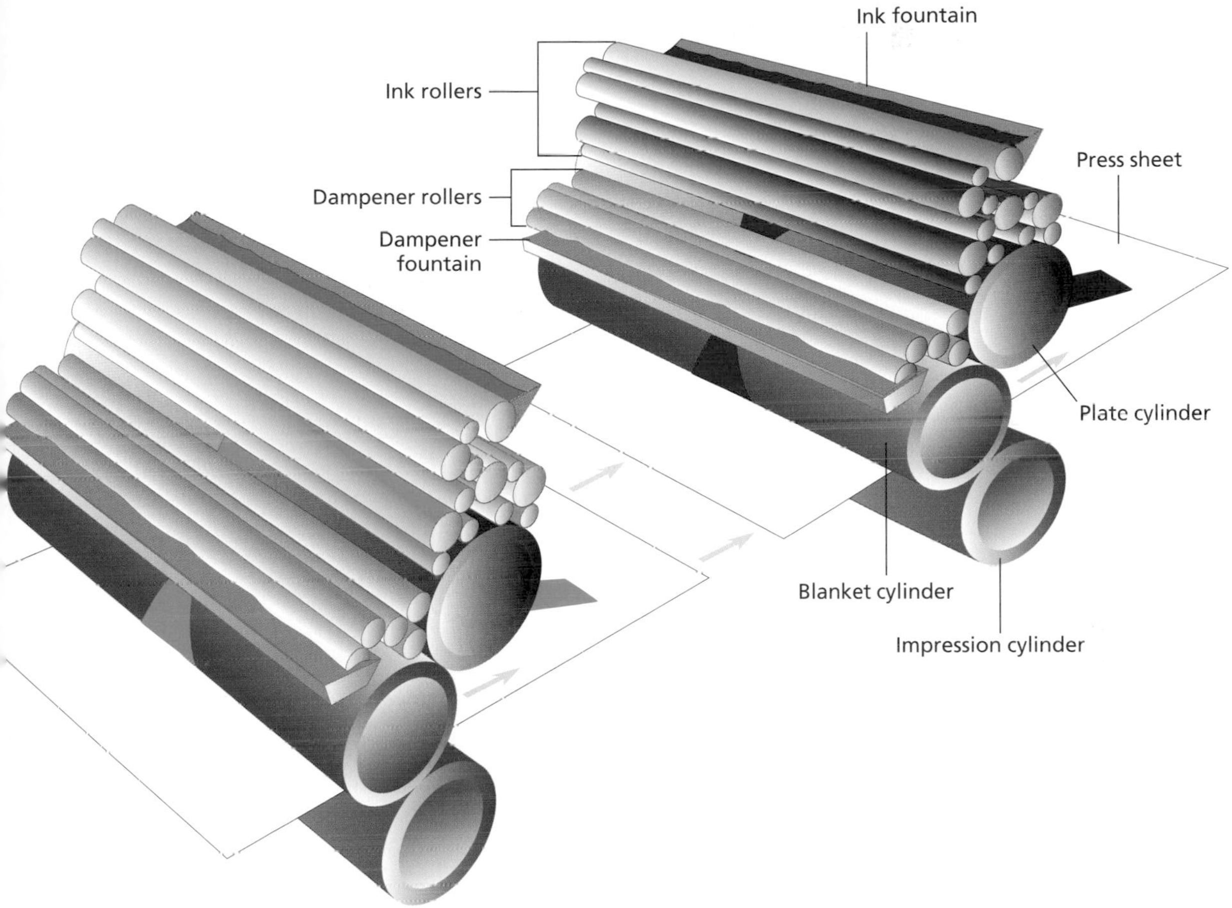

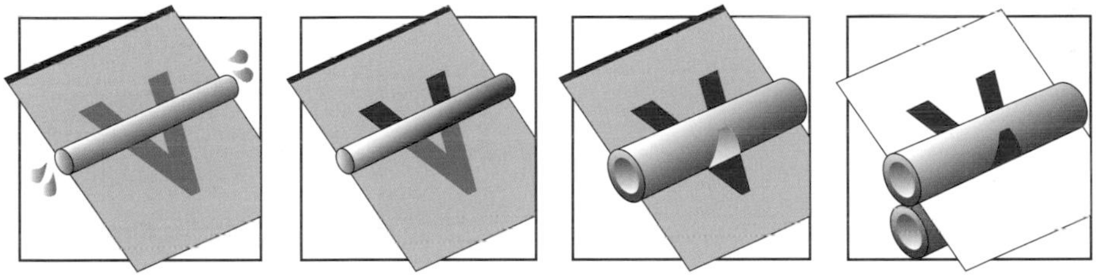

1. The plate is dampened by the dampener rollers. The image area repels water.

2. Ink rollers apply ink to the "oleophilic" (image) areas on the plate.

3. Ink is transferred from the plate cylinder to the blanket cylinder. The water stays behind.

4. The blanket cylinder transfers ink to the press sheet.

Other Printing Processes

Flexography

Flexography uses a raised-image plate made of flexible photopolymer or rubber that prints directly onto a printing substrate. The flexible plate makes it possible to print on irregular surfaces such as pressure-sensitive label paper, plastic films, and corrugated cardboard. Because of the soft plates, flexography generates greater dot gain. Ink coverage on flexographic presses is defined by a special ink roller called the *anilox roller.*

Flexographic printing is required for some food packaging—it's the only printing process that can print on materials that come in contact with food. It's also common for printing on pressure-sensitive labels, shrink-plastics used on beverage bottles, and pharmaceutical products.

Intaglio printing (gravure)

Intaglio printing uses an engraved plate that carries the image. *Flat* intaglio printing usually goes by the name *engraved printing* and is used for fine business and personal stationery and announcements. *Rotary* intaglio printing is called *rotogravure*; it's used for very-long-run commercial printing jobs like magazines and catalogs.

For rotogravure, the image is engraved on a copper cylinder; the surface of the plate represents the nonprinting areas. The plate cylinder rotates in a bath of ink, and the ink is retained in the engraved cells of the plate. As it turns, the cylinder comes in contact with a *doctor blade,* which removes the ink from the nonimage areas (like a squeegee). The cylinder then transfers the ink to the paper against an impression cylinder.

The cost of preparing rotogravure cylinders for printing and then doing the printing requires that this process be used for projects that run in the millions of impressions.

The quality of rotogravure printing is excellent, delivering some of the nicest results in the world. Publications like *National Geographic* magazine are printed using this process.

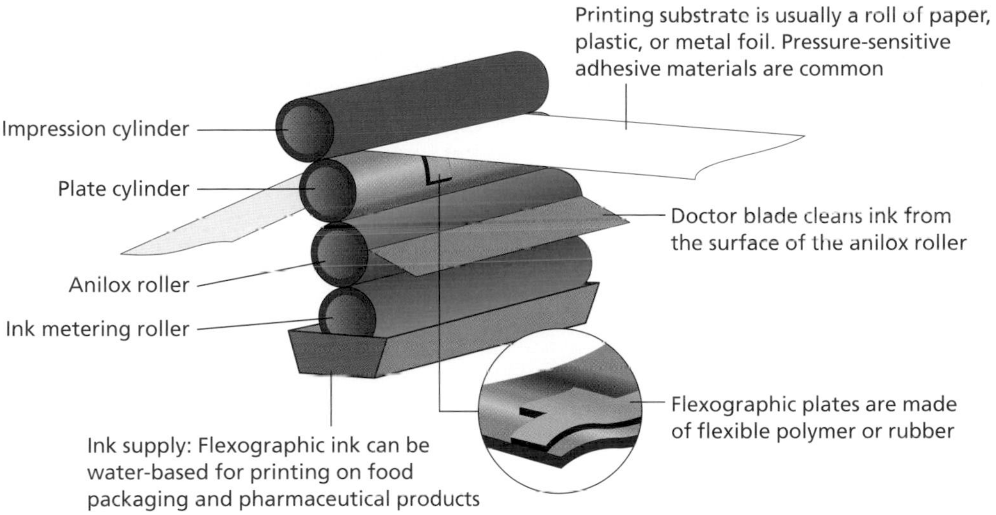
Printing substrate is usually a roll of paper, plastic, or metal foil. Pressure-sensitive adhesive materials are common
Impression cylinder
Plate cylinder
Doctor blade cleans ink from the surface of the anilox roller
Anilox roller
Ink metering roller
Flexographic plates are made of flexible polymer or rubber
Ink supply: Flexographic ink can be water-based for printing on food packaging and pharmaceutical products

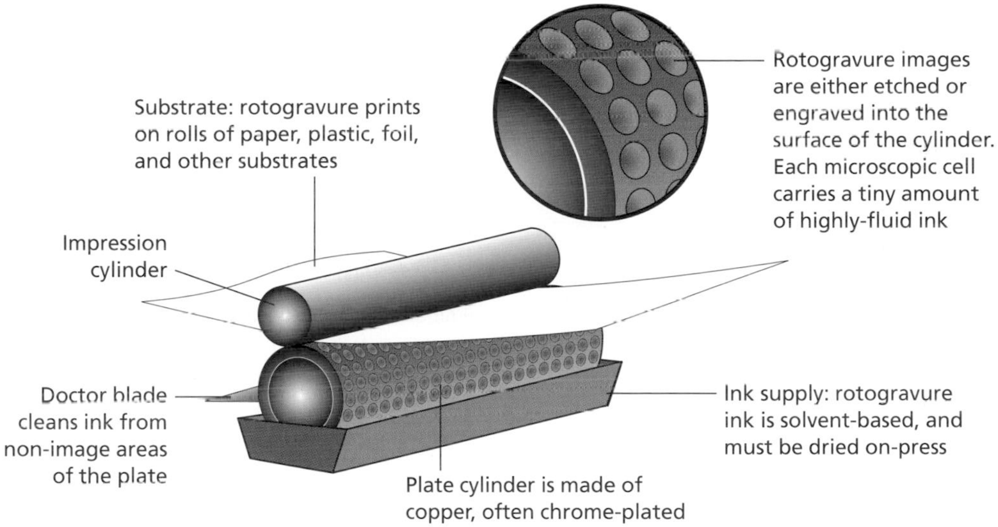
Rotogravure images are either etched or engraved into the surface of the cylinder. Each microscopic cell carries a tiny amount of highly-fluid ink
Substrate: rotogravure prints on rolls of paper, plastic, foil, and other substrates
Impression cylinder
Doctor blade cleans ink from non-image areas of the plate
Ink supply: rotogravure ink is solvent-based, and must be dried on-press
Plate cylinder is made of copper, often chrome-plated

Screen printing

Screen printing is the relatively simple method of forcing ink through a screen stencil and onto a printable surface. Because screen printing lays down the ink up to 30 times thicker than lithography, the color is more dense and durable than it is in other printing processes. Screen printing uses photographically prepared stencils to transfer designs onto almost any surface, including posters, clothing, compact discs, and bottles. The screens are exposed from film positives made on an imagesetter.

Screen printing on fabrics may require using larger traps to compensate for misregister. A relatively low screen ruling of 35–55 lines per inch is appropriate for printing on textiles. One of the attractions of screen printing is the great variety of inks possible, including glittered and fluorescent inks.

Specialty printing and finishing

After printing, a number of processes can enhance the appearance of a product, including the application of varnishes, aqueous coatings, foil stamping, embossing, die-cutting, and thermography. *Varnishes*, which are clear or tinted inks, are usually applied on the same press that does the printing, but these coatings can also be added after printing. Varnishes and coatings can cover entire sheets or can be used to print over parts of a printed project to enhance its appearance. Many designers use varnish to augment the appearance of photos in a publication.

Relief printing processes add metallic or colored foil, patterns, raised panels, or raised lettering to the printed sheet. Most of these processes require the manufacture of a metal printing die (and sometimes a counter-die), but the cost of these tools isn't extravagant. Other than the expense of the dies, finishing operations like these add just a few pennies to the cost of each printed piece.

Thermography is a finishing process that uses plastic resin to add an embossed effect to printing. After the ink is printed on the paper, it's dusted with powdered resin, which sticks to the ink. The surface passes under a vacuum cleaner to remove the unused powder and then under a flash-heater, which causes the powdered resin to boil. The image rises in relief to produce an interesting effect. This process is often used to print business cards, stationery, invitations, and greeting cards.

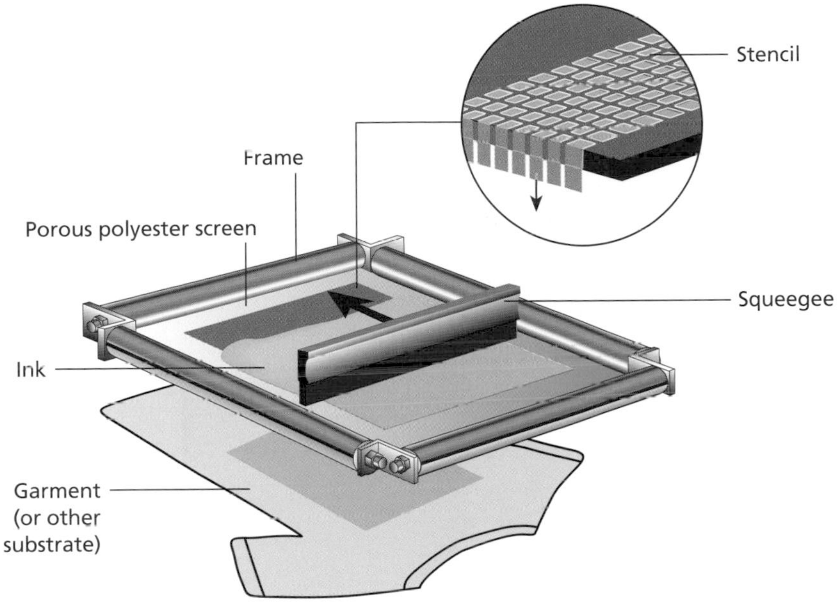
Stencil
Frame
Porous polyester screen
Squeegee
Ink
Garment
(or other
substrate)

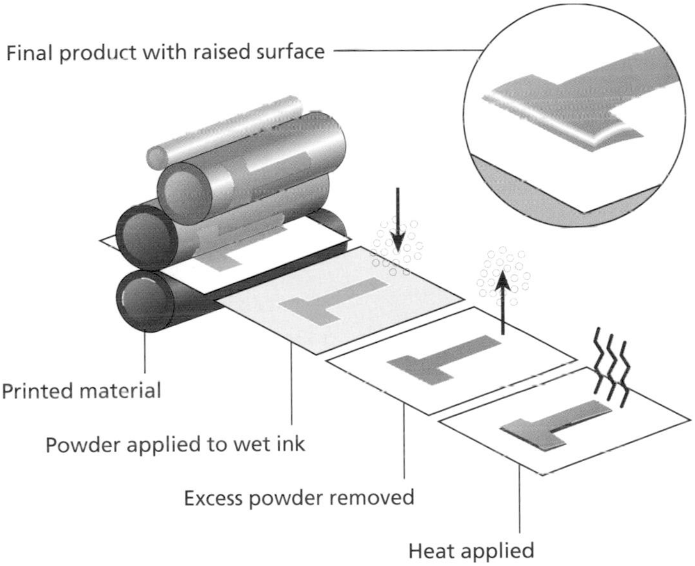
Final product with raised surface
Printed material
Powder applied to wet ink
Excess powder removed
Heat applied

Printing Terms

Aqueous coating Some printing presses have an extra unit for adding an aqueous (water-based) varnish to an entire sheet as it is printed. These coatings add a lovely gloss to a printed piece and make them more durable and less prone to fingerprints and smudges.

Anilox The flexographic printing process requires a special roller to control the density of the ink transferred from the ink metering roller to the printing plate. Anilox rollers are cylinders with microscopic cells etched into the surface. Each cell has a fixed volume, which defines the amount of ink the cell can hold. A *doctor blade* removes ink from the surface of the anilox as it turns.

Blanket In offset printing, a rubberized surface that transfers the inked image from plate to paper.

Blanket cylinder In offset presses, the metal cylinder around which the blanket is wrapped.

Cold-set printing Ink applied to paper on a printing press, then allowed to air-dry by evaporation of the *vehicle* that made the ink liquid. As opposed to *heat-set* printing, where the ink is dried by heating elements in the printing press.

Cover stock Heavy-weight paper used for the covers of magazines and publications.

Dampening In lithography, fountain solution (mostly water) is applied to the plate as it turns. Image areas are smooth (called *oleophilic*), which makes them attractive to ink. Non-image areas are porous (called *hydrophilic*), which makes them attractive to water. When in balance, the ink sticks to the smooth areas and the water to the porous areas.

Densitometer A device used to measure the density of ink (the ink film thickness). Density is the inverse of reflectivity.

Die A stamping tool used in embossing and cutting. Often requires a counter-die.

Dimensional stability A paper's resistance to stretching or distortion, especially when damp.

Doctor blade A siff squeegee-like blade that removes excess ink on flexographic and gravure printing presses.

Dot gain The spread of dots during several stages of printing or platemaking, as measured by the increase in size of a midtone dot. When a 50% dot expands into a 60% dot, the gain is 10%. *Average* dot gain on offset printing is more than 20%. All printing processes experience dot gain, even ink-jet and toner-based printing.

Dry lithography and waterless offset A type of lithographic printing that uses a plate with a coating that repels ink without needing to be dampened. Ink is confined to the image area without the usual dampening. These plates are usually surfaced with silicone in the non-image areas.

Drying oven An oven used to dry paper after printing. In heat-set web-offset lithography, the paper passes from the press through a drying oven on its way to the folding and finishing units on the press.

Embossing Producing a raised image in paper by means of a die striking from the back of the paper into a counter-die at the front.

Engraving (Intaglio) A printing process in the family of Intaglio printing, where the image is engraved into a copper or steel plate. On the press, the plate is cleaned by a squeegee (*doctor*) blade, and the ink is then transferred by pressure and capillary action. Engraving is used for fine business stationery and currency printing.

Flexography Relief printing using a flexible printing plate—usually a photopolymer. The image is raised, as with an ordinary letterpress. Flexography is most commonly used to print on food product labels , pressure-sensitive labels, cardboard and other packaging.

Form A form is one side of a *signature.* A group of pages positioned so that when folded and finished, they come out in the right order and position.

Fountain The supply of ink for a lithographic press. Sometimes also the supply of dampening solution.

Gang run Two or more printing jobs run simultaneously on the same press sheet. Large sheets of paper are shared by several jobs and, after printing, are cut into separate jobs.

Gravure printing (Intaglio) Sometimes called *engraved printing,* gravure is printing by the Intaglio process where the image is engraved into a copper plate, ink is applied, then the residue is removed from the surface by a stiff blade called a *doctor blade.* This is the process used to print fine business stationery and currency. A variant is *rotogravure,* used to print very-long-run publications like the *National Geographic.*

Gripper edge The gripper edge of a sheet of paper is the leading edge where the sheet is grasped mechanically and drawn into the press.

Gripper margin Unprinted space allowed along the gripper edge of the printing medium.

Halo effect Occurs when ink builds up at the edge of an area, making the interior look lighter. Common in electrophotographic (toner) printing and some letterpress.

Hickey A donut-shaped imperfection in presswork caused by paper particles that get stuck to the blanket cylinder of an offset press.

Imposition The arrangement of pages for printing on a press sheet in such a way that they appear in correct order when the sheet is folded.

Impression cylinder A cylinder that presses paper into contact with an inked surface.

Ink coverage A percentage indicating the inked area of the paper. Also called *dot area,* it is the ratio of area covered by ink divided into the area measured.

Printing Terms (continued)

Inkometer A tool for measuring the tackiness or stickiness of ink.

Inner form The part of an imposition that consists of inside pages. On a printed sheet, the inner form pages are those that will be on the inside when the sheet is folded into a signature.

Intaglio A family of printing processes where the image is engraved *into* the printing plate. Used primarily by two printing processes: *gravure* printing—used for fine stationery and currency printing, and *rotogravure,* used to print very long runs of commercial publications. The benefits include tremendous ink film thickness and the run-length of the plates, which will last for millions of impressions.

Lay-down sequence The order in which colors are printed.

Letterpress Relief printing directly onto the paper. The oldest form of printing. Raised areas of the plate hold the ink and transfer it directly. This is in contrast to intaglio or gravure printing, where sunken recesses hold the ink, and also in contrast to offset printing, where the plate has no relief.

Letterset Offset-letterpress printing. The image is defined by raised areas, as in the direct case. The raised areas get inked but do not come in contact with the paper. Instead, the image is transferred to a blanket, which in turn transfers it to paper. Also called *dry offset*. Resembles offset lithography in using a blanket as intermediary.

Moiré pattern Any of several interference patterns that show up in printed products a result of the *nearly exact* frequency of halftone dot patterns with other patterns in the artwork. Moiré is known by physicists as a *beat pattern* where two similar patterns occasionally match but not consistently, causing a visible wave-like pattern in an image.

Offset Printing that uses an intermediary surface called a blanket to transfer the image from the inked surface to the paper.

Perfector A type of printing press that prints both sides of the paper as it passes through the press. Web presses are usually capable of perfecting the job as it is printed.

Photopolymer plate Most flexographic printing is done with a relatively thin plate made of a polymer material and coated with a photosensitive surface, which is exposed from a film negative and processed to create a relief image. Rubber plates are used in some flexographic operations.

Piling A printing problem in which ink pigment accumulates on a plate or blanket.

Platen press A type of flat letterpress that uses a hinged clamping action to bring the paper and plate together.

Press proof A proof pulled from the press prior to an actual print run.

Press run or print run The number of copies in one printing.

Progressive proofs, or progs Proofs made on a press. Each color is shown separately, and various combinations are shown overprinted. Progs are used as a guide in adjusting the final color quality.

Register The correct alignment of colors during printing.

Register mark A mark to assist in making the correct alignment of overlay copy and color during printing in multiple colors.

Relief plate A printing plate with a raised, image-bearing surface. Letterpress and flexography use a relief plate.

Rotary printing Any method using a cylinder as the primary printing surface.

Rotogravure Intaglio printing on a rotary, web-fed press.

Rubber plate A flexible relief plate used in flexography.

Screen printing A process in the *porous* family of printing processes. Used to print on garments, industrial products, and signs, screen printing is capable of laying down a tremendous amount of ink. The process involves making a stencil with fabric and a photo-sensitive coating, and using very thick plastic ink and a squeegee to force the ink through the stencil onto the substrate.

Sheet-fed press A printing press into which individual sheets of paper are fed, as contrasted with a *web-fed* press printing on a continuous roll of material—usually paper.

Show-through When the impression on one side of a sheet is visible on the other side, through the paper.

Signature A group of pages printed on the same sheet, front and back. After printing, the sheet is folded so that the pages fall in correct order.

Slurring A printing problem in which halftone dots appear elongated or smeared.

Tack Adhesive quality, or stickiness, of ink.

Trim marks Marks indicating where to trim.

Varnish A clear or tinted ink that adds a sheen or gloss or even a matte-surface quality to the press sheet. Varnish usually requires an extra printing plate with images for the desired areas to be coated. See also *aqueous coating*.

Web-fed press A printing press into which a continuous roll of paper is fed.

Work-and-tumble A type of sheet-fed printing in which front and back images share a single plate. The sheet is printed on one side, flipped end-to-end (along the gripper-edge axis), and printed on the other side. After flipping, the paper has a new gripper-edge.

Work-and-turn Another type of sheet-fed printing in which front and back images share a single plate. The sheet is printed on one side and then turned side-to-side so that the back side can be printed with the same plate. This does not change the paper's gripper-edge.

Zinc engravings Line or halftone art as a relief image on zinc plates for letterpress printing. Other metals have also been used in the making of relief plates: aluminum, magnesium, copper, and brass.

Imposition and Binding

Most printing presses print large sheets of paper. *Imposition* is the process of arranging the pages of a publication so that when the sheets are printed and folded for binding, the pages are in the proper sequence.

Each press sheet is called a *signature*. Each side of the signature is called a *form*. The signature is bound with others as necessary and trimmed to create a finished publication.

The arrangement of pages for a form is usually done with imposition software in the printing plant. A *folding dummy* is constructed to model the final piece, and then information about the job's folding requirements are put into the imposition software. The imposition software rearranges the pages in a document into the right order and orientation for printing and then sends the forms to the platesetter for imaging.

Binding is the process of gathering folded signatures using one of several methods. In *saddle-stitch* binding, signatures are gathered to form a common spine and then stitched with staples made from wire on the machine. *Perfect* binding involves gathering groups of signatures, grinding the bound edge to create a strong binding surface, and gluing the signatures at the spine with a hot-melt glue into a one-piece paper cover.

When signatures are folded, the inner pages of each move outward slightly. The more pages a signature contains, the farther the pages closest to the center of the signature move with respect to the other pages. This phenomenon is known as *creep*. The imposition software can compensate for creep by moving the pages of a signature inward in minute increments so that the trimmed signature doesn't have an obvious image movement from the ends to the middle.

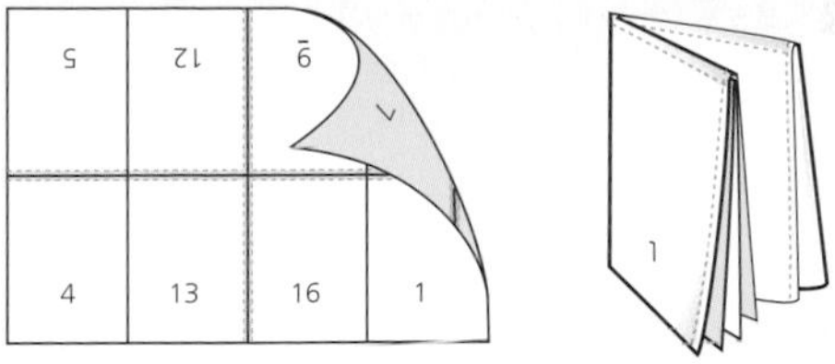

Imposed 16-page signature and folded signature

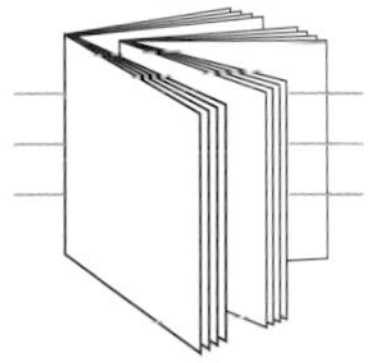

Inserted signatures

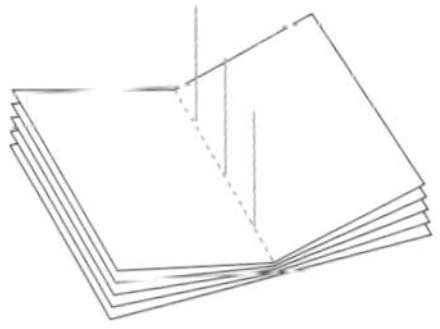

Saddle-stitch binding

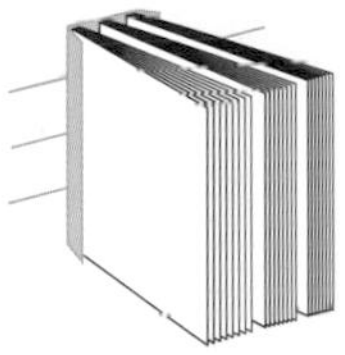

Gathered signatures

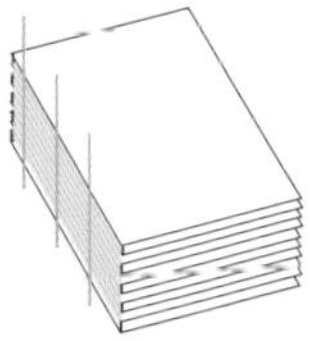

Perfect binding

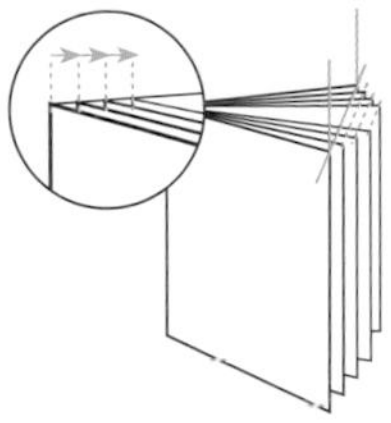

Creep occurs when the inner pages of a signature project outwards.

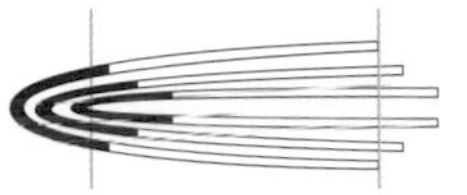

Creep affects the printed area during binding and trimming

Binding and Finishing Terms

Accordion fold Parallel folds, alternating in direction. Also called *concertina fold.*

Binding Any of many processes used to assemble pages or signatures.

Collate To gather pages in a particular order for binding.

Die A stamping tool used in embossing and cutting.

Die-cutting Cutting a paper product with a die. This usually refers to steel-rule die-cutting, where shaped cuts are made to printed products on a letterpress machine. Common uses include cutting slits for a business card to be inserted on a booklet, or cutting the flaps on pocket-folders. Flexographic printing uses rotary die-cutting, which is done on the printing press. Rotary dies are capable of intricate detail and extraordinary precision.

Embossing Producing a raised image in paper by means of a die striking from the back of the paper into a counter-die at the front. Embossing can be simple, called *blind-embossing,* where the paper is squeezed in the die-counter-die pair, causing an image or shape to be raised. Embossing can also be more complex, involving colored or metallic foils, or textures and heat, each of which imparts an image with both relief and color.

Endpapers The heavy paper at the front and back of a book, to which coverboard is glued. They hold the body of a book into the covers.

Form A form is one side of a *signature.* A group of pages positioned so that when folded and finished, they come out in the right order and position.

Glue binding A method of binding that depends on glue, also called *perfect* binding.

Jogging Vibrating a stack of sheets before binding or trimming. Used to bring the edges in-line.

Perfect binding An unsewn, flat-spined binding made with glue. Also called a *glue binding.*

Saddle-stitching A type of binding that uses wire stapling at the center of a magazine or pamphlet. Folded spreads are placed over a peaked frame called a saddle and stapled through the middle. The "stitches" are staples made from a roll of wire on the binding machine.

Side-stitching A method of binding that involves stapling through the spine of a publication from front to back. This prevents the book from lying flat when it is opened.

Signature A group of pages printed on the same sheet, front and back. After printing, the sheet is folded so that the pages fall in correct order.

Spine The backbone of a book, particularly of the binding.

Thermography An embossed effect obtained by applying resinous powder to a wet image and fusing it with heat.

Everything I've learned about printing:

Keep an open mind; stay proactive; pick your battles; what you don't know learn; it's okay if the printed piece looks better than the proof; attitude is everything; and finally, as with this quote, no matter how much time you have to produce a piece, it always comes down to the wire.

—Gina Long, Lithomania, Inc., South San Francisco, CA

2 Constructing a Publication

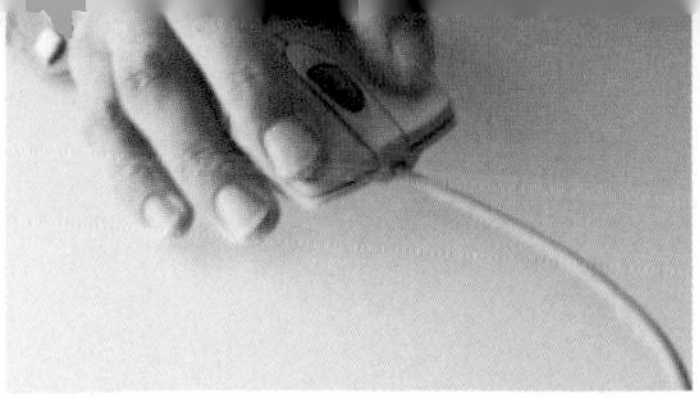

Constructing a Publication

The way you create your publication isn't only critical to the success of your design—it also affects the way your publication prints. This chapter covers the issues involved in creating a publication for commercial printing, such as creating page layouts that avoid typical printing pitfalls, choosing the best file formats, and compensating for register error using overprinting or trapping. When properly assembled, a publication will print correctly and require less rework for you and your vendors.

Guidelines for Specifying Colors

You can specify colors either by referring to a printed color swatch book or by using a calibrated computer display and selecting colors onscreen.

When you use an illustration program to create art that will later be used in your page layout, be sure to use the same color names in both applications. For example, if you use *Pantone 228 C* in your Adobe Illustrator document, the color will be named the same when the art is placed in your Adobe InDesign layout and will have the same display characteristics. It's wise to double-check the color palette in your page layout application to be sure that spot colors aren't duplicated. If they are, be sure to consolidate them by deleting one of the duplicates and assigning all items that use that color to the other similarly named color.

Whether you use spot colors, process colors, or a combination of both in your publication depends on your budget, the purpose of the publication, the type of page elements you use, and how your design will be reproduced. Use the following guidelines to determine what colors are suitable for your publication.

Use spot colors when:

- You need one or two colors, and you won't be reproducing full-color photographs.
- You want the effect of special inks, such as metallic, fluorescent, or corporate color inks. These are often colors that can't be reproduced with combinations of the process colors.
- You want to print logos or other graphics elements that require precise color matching, or you're printing large areas of color throughout a publication and you want to ensure color consistency.

Use process colors when:

- You need more than two colors in your publication. Printing with process color inks (CMYK) costs less than printing with three or more spot inks. (Printers usually print with process colors; to print in spot colors requires a different press setup, which takes time and costs money.)
- You want to reproduce full-color photographs or color artwork that can only be reproduced with process colors.

Use spot and process colors together when:

- Your requirements extend beyond process color printing. This could involve corporate colors, as already explained, or extending the range of process color by using a *bump plate*—a spot color plate that serves to intensify one of the process colors. Remember that printing with more than four inks can be expensive because of the extra plates and press work.

earth & ware
the gardener's catalog
Purpose & longevity separate an ordinary gadget from the invaluable tool.
MUCH LIKE A WELL-APPOINTED KITCHEN, A GOOD SHED IS FILLED ONLY WITH THE ESSENTIALS—THOSE TOOLS THAT TURN TIRESOME CHORES INTO SIMPLE TASKS. WITH ROUTINE CARE, ALL OUR PRODUCTS PROMISE A LIFETIME OF USE.
boots
favorite essentials
shovels
enhance the flavor of your meals with a selection of herbs from Earth & Ware. While fall is usually reserved for yard work and preparation for the colder months ahead, it's also the perfect time to let herb plants mature indoors.
organic herbs
spring seedling basket
fresh herbs
Color photograph printed with process inks
Vector art using a spot color
Rich black display type using black and magenta process inks
Spot varnish applied to enhance the text effect
Text with spot color applied

Specifying spot colors and varnishes

Specifying a spot color means that any page element assigned that color or any screened tint of that color will appear on its own printing plate. Name spot colors consistently across all the applications you're using, including illustration, photo-editing, and page-layout programs.

Remember that when you're printing with spot colors, the name you assign to a color doesn't determine what ink will be used on press. But naming colors consistently helps ensure that your artwork will separate correctly and reduces the chance of confusion between you and your printer. You specify which spot inks should be used when you submit your files to the printer.

If your artwork contains both spot and process colors, you can convert spot colors to their process-color equivalents; doing so lets you print with four process colors and thereby save money. When you convert a spot color into a process color, be aware that most spot colors can't be reproduced accurately with process inks. When you convert spot colors to their process color equivalents in computer applications, consider the components of the resulting colors, and look for opportunities to simplify them.

For example, specifying Pantone 406 C (a light gray) and then converting that gray into process colors creates a combination of 1 percent cyan, 5 percent magenta, 6 percent yellow, and 16 percent black. It isn't a good idea to have a 1 percent cyan value in a critical color, because that color can be lost in platemaking or can cause color balance and register problems on-press. It's better to eliminate the cyan component of the color.

Varnishes are used to protect a page, to create a visual effect, or to emphasize photographs or other elements of a publication. Varnish can be applied to whole pages of the publication or applied only to specific areas. As an alternative to a printed varnish, some presses have the option of applying an aqueous coating that covers the whole press sheet, creating a handsome gloss veneer.

Specify a spot varnish just as you would a spot color. If you want to print varnish over photographs, you must create a duplicate of your page layout document, delete the photos from their frames, and then set the frames to be filled with the varnish color. The printer will generate a separate printing plate from the duplicate document for the varnish panels that overprint the photos. Varnish used elsewhere in a document should be included in the layout and separated with the varnish used over the photos. If varnish is used in a layout, it's generally set to overprint.

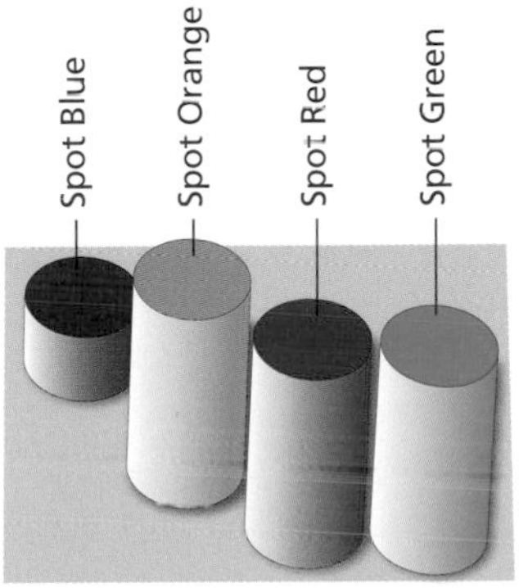

Spot color (simulated)

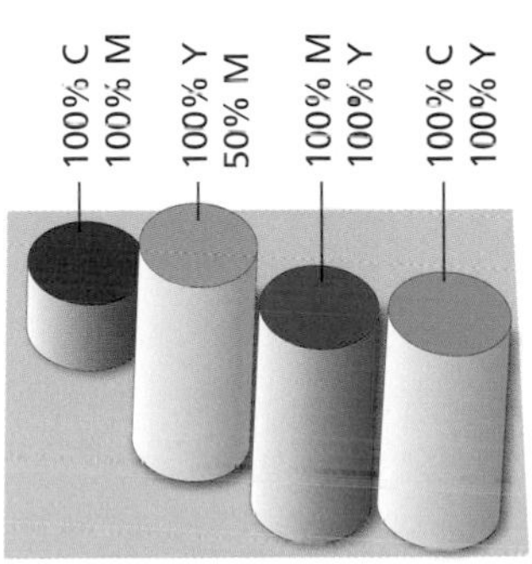

Spot color converted to process

Publication page

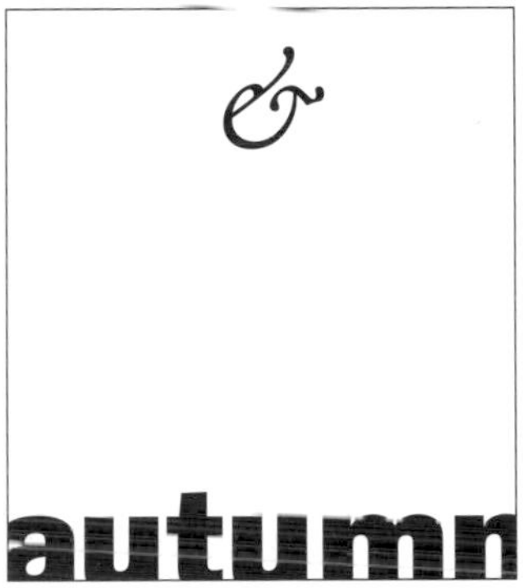

Varnish silhouette

50% screen

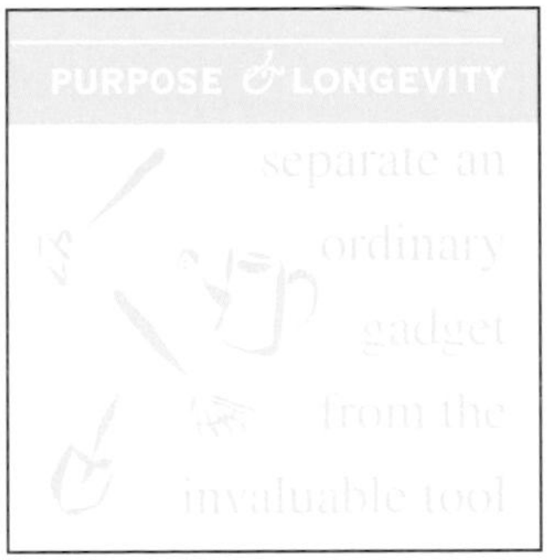

100% screen

Specifying process colors

To achieve predictable printed results, it's a good idea to select colors from one of the commercial process-color swatch books available. Remember that paper surface affects the character of ink and thus the color reproduced by process colors. So, printed colors may not look exactly the way they do in the swatch book.

Because process black is transparent, the addition of another process color to black is often beneficial. A *rich black* ink combines process black ink with one or more of the other process inks to achieve a more intense black. Use a rich black in areas where objects could show through process black and cause it to appear inconsistent or not dense enough.

Use a single, solid ink (such as 100 percent black or a dark spot color) to print hairline rules and small text. Fine elements printed with two or more colors are difficult to print in register.

Avoid creating process colors with high total ink coverage (the sum of the percentages of the four process colors). Most paper and press conditions require a maximum ink coverage of 250–320 percent. Higher total ink coverage may prevent the ink from drying correctly and can cause *set-off,* where the ink from one sheet of paper is transferred to the next sheet in the pile. Your printer will know the total ink coverage limit for their press and paper combinations.

Process black (100% K)

Rich black created with 100% K + 20% C + 20% M + 20% Y

Cool rich black created with 100% K + 20% C

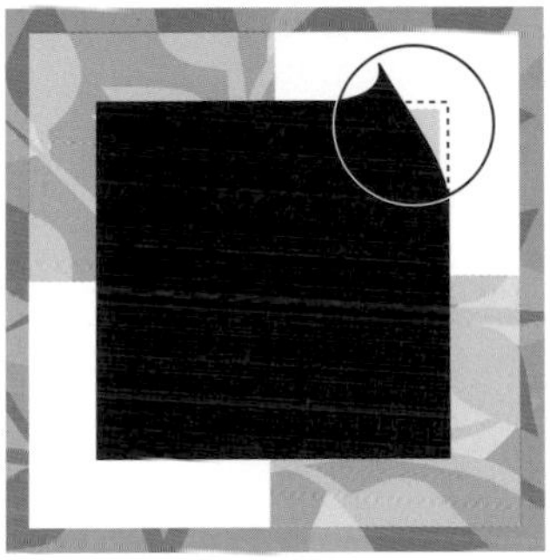

Warm rich black created with 100% K + 20% M

Process colors in small type and fine elements are more likely to show register error on press.

Black or spot colors in small type and fine elements produce a sharp edge.

Using a Color Management System

A color management system is used to achieve color consistency between different devices. Ideally, this means the colors on your computer display accurately represent both the colors in the digital image and the colors you'll see in your publication when it's printed. If a system-wide color management system is in use, you can achieve accurate color matching through all stages of the production process and in multiple contexts, including Web publications, composite color proofs, and final printed products.

Color management relies on an industry standard color profile format developed by the International Color Consortium (ICC). With color management, a software application saves color files with embedded ICC color profiles. The application also reads ICC profiles when it opens a color file. Adobe Photoshop, Illustrator, InDesign, and QuarkXPress all support color management to help ensure consistent color as files move between these applications and various proofing and printing devices.

For color management to work effectively, all applications you use to process a color file must support color management, and ICC profiles must be available for all output devices you use. If you plan to choose colors on your computer display, the computer display must be calibrated and have an ICC profile set.

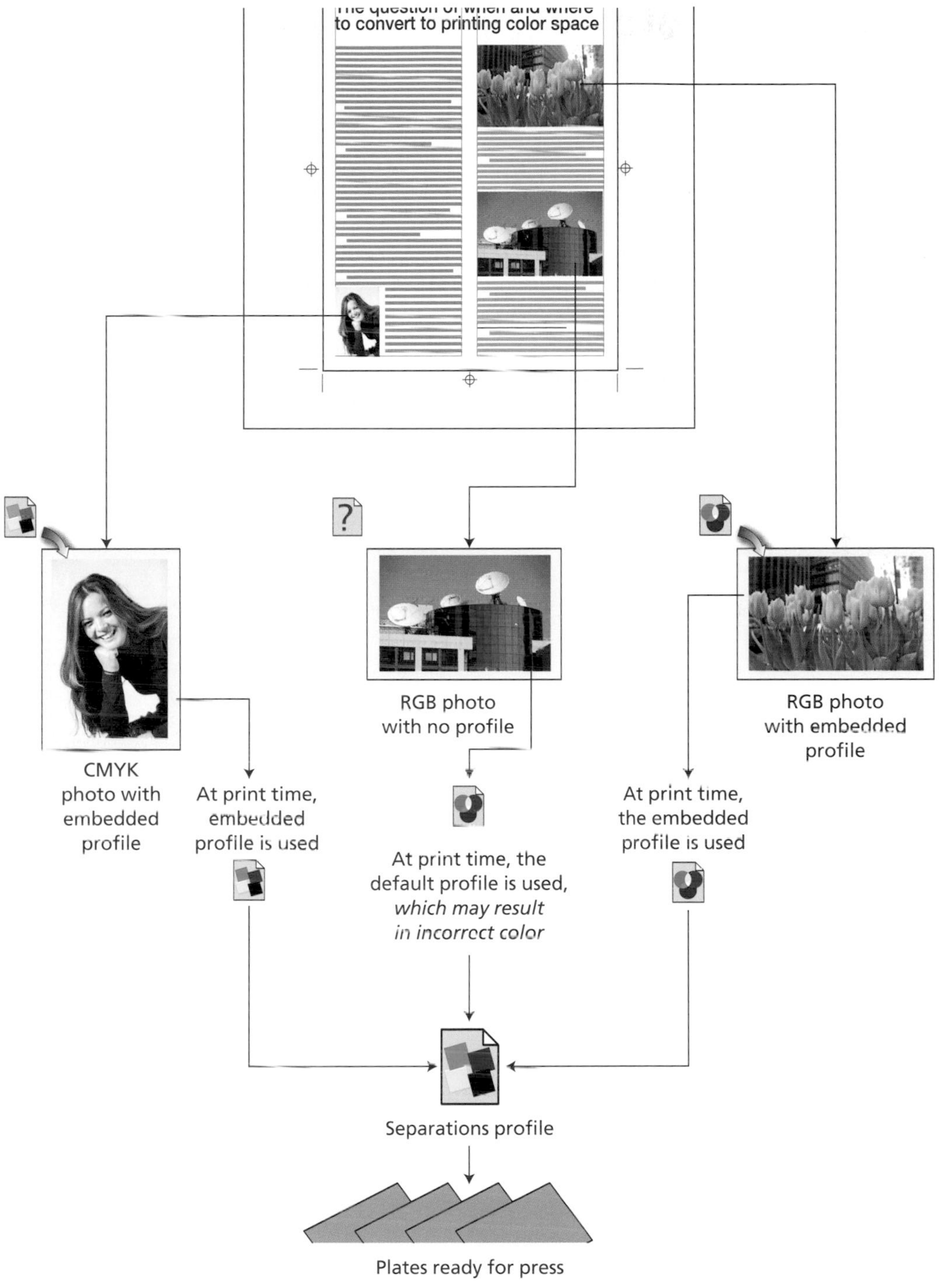
to convert to printing color space
CMYK photo with embedded profile
RGB photo with no profile
RGB photo with embedded profile
At print time, embedded profile is used
At print time, the default profile is used, *which may result in incorrect color*
At print time, the embedded profile is used
Separations profile
Plates ready for press

Using a Color Management System (continued)

If your prepress service provider uses color management, be sure to discuss the best way to ensure your project is produced effectively. Depending on your printer's preferred workflow, it may be possible for your layout to contain images and illustrations in a variety of color spaces—RGB, CMYK, or grayscale—and have the conversion to output color done by the printer at the time of output. The benefit of this procedure is that one master page layout can be created without regard for the output process or medium. The output is optimized according to the process used.

Commercial printing companies that have adopted color management usually have ICC profiles available for their printing processes. They will provide these profiles to you on request, and the profile appropriate to your project can be used to make an onscreen preview of the printing.

Photoshop embeds its color working space profile into images as they are saved in most file formats. This color space is an ICC profile that defines the gamut of colors inside of which the image exists. Most consumer digital cameras—and all professional digital cameras—also embed a color profile into images as they are saved to memory cards.

Color-managed workflows acknowledge these color profiles when processing images and can convert the colors in the image more accurately to destination color spaces—like CMYK—when these profiles are present. Some experts refer to embedded ICC profiles as the *pedigree* of images, helping to define their character as they are processed for printing.

If your printer prefers that all color in a document be converted to CMYK in advance of printing, then it's important to get a CMYK press profile from the printer to use in converting to their color requirements. If the printer doesn't provide a process-specific profile, ask for their recommendation of a CMYK profile that is acceptable to them. The Adobe Creative Suite ships with a number of CMYK profiles that are useful for converting color to CMYK for web-fed and sheet-fed processes.

The "Digital Age" has empowered designers to create their own images, set their own type, and even make their own traps. It also makes us more liable for potential printing errors than ever before. Knowing your tools and how to use them has never been more essential.

—Clifford Stoltze, Stoltze Design, Boston, MA

Correcting Color

It may be necessary to correct the color in an image that's scanned or that comes from a digital camera. The original photograph may have a color cast caused by using incorrect film or lighting. Or, the scan may have been imperfect—some scanners introduce color casts in images. Or perhaps the colors in your original art are out of gamut for the printing process, and you want to modify a color in the original to make it printable.

If you're using professionally scanned images, you can often avoid the need to correct the color if you discuss your requirements with the scanner operator. A skilled scanner operator who knows what you want can eliminate color cast in the original.

Photoshop includes numerous color-correction tools and many techniques for making images perfect for print.

Choice of color mode

Color can be corrected in either RGB or CMYK mode. For a variety of reasons, it's advisable to do most retouching and color correction work in RGB. The number of tools, filters, and functions available in Photoshop is greatest when you're working in this mode. Even Selective Color, a CMYK-based color correction tool, works in RGB mode.

Working in RGB color

All digital photographs and most scanned images are in RGB color. And as just mentioned, most experts believe it's best to do corrections and editing in RGB mode. It's best to leave images in their original color space and perform editing and color correction on the images in that space.

RGB gives you greater flexibility in how you use images. For example, an image may appear in a newspaper ad, a high-quality brochure, a poster printed using European-standard inks, or on the Web. By comparison, color images in CMYK mode are device specific; once you've converted to CMYK, you're locked into using a particular printing process and substrate.

Converting from one color mode to another can be harmful to an image, and it's best not to convert more than once. Using embedded ICC profiles allows images to remain in RGB color and then be converted to printing color (CMYK or other) at print time, leaving the color in the original unchanged. Such workflows provide the greatest amount of flexibility.

Working in CMYK color

A CMYK image is process-specific—it's optimized for output to a particular printing device, ink set, and substrate. This means that colors and the tonal range have been changed (or limited) to fit those of the printing device.

As mentioned in the previous section, you should avoid switching color modes. If you're starting with a professional scan delivered in CMYK, it's best to stay in that mode all the way through production. If you start with an

RGB scan and perform the major part of the job in RGB, you still have the option of doing fine-tuning with Photoshop's CMYK color-correction tools.

Working in CMYK has some advantages: You can specify and measure definite CMYK color values as percentages, and they don't change. If you want 100 percent cyan, for example, you can be sure of getting that value.

Using levels and curves

Photoshop provides a histogram (Image > Adjustments > Levels) for image editing. A *histogram* shows the number of pixels at each brightness level in the image. A broad histogram is usually desirable; a narrow histogram indicates that the image has a narrow tonal range. A histogram that is concentrated at either the dark end or the light end can indicate a number of problems—underexposure, poor contrast, or poor original lighting.

You can make changes in the image by adjusting the sliders below the histogram. The left end represents the darkest areas of an image, and the right end represents the lightest areas. The slider in the middle lets you adjust the image's contrast and saturation.

Many professionals use the histogram to analyze their images and adjust the end points (black and white). They then use a different control—Curves—to make additional adjustments for brightness and contrast. Curves has the advantage of allowing control over more tonal points in the image.

Both Levels (showing the histogram) and Curves can control the entire image or individual color channels. You can use these controls to modify the color in an image. Practicing with a number of images will help you develop the color-correction skills to fix nearly any image.

CMYK preview

Even when you're working with RGB or Lab color images, Photoshop lets you preview images in CMYK, according to its current Color Settings (and additional custom settings). If you want to see the impact of conversion to CMYK, without the commitment to convert, use Preview.

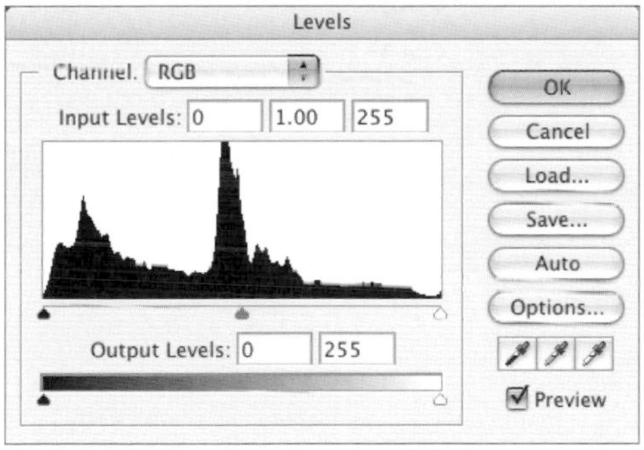

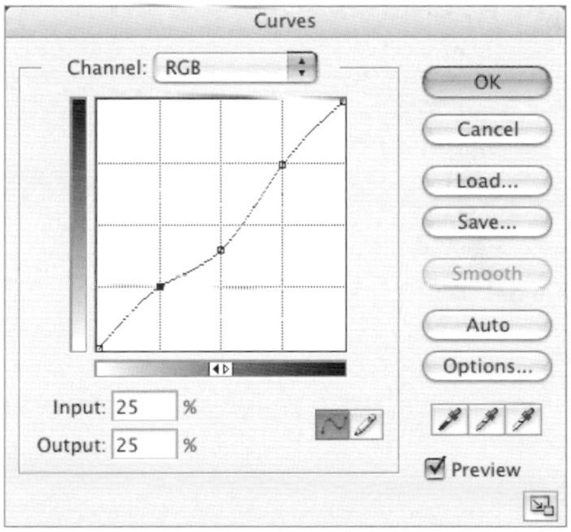

Color-correction in Photoshop

Each time you adjust color in Photoshop, the data in your file is permanently altered. Thus, your goal during correction and editing should be to perform as few adjustments as you need to achieve the results you want. Over-editing and overcorrection may result in a degradation of image quality.

By contrast, *layer effects* in Photoshop are nondestructive and can be cancelled or changed at any time. Most imaging professionals use these layer effects to experiment and change images with the confidence that their changes can be removed if they wish.

Photoshop has a number of color-correction tools, including a series of color palettes based on lighting conditions. Fixing digital photos taken under incorrect lighting conditions is the most common correction—and one of the easiest—to perform. And if you have a digital camera that can deliver an image in *raw* format, you can correct the image's color for color temperature down to the degree as it's opened in Photoshop.

One of the simplest methods for color-correcting images in Photoshop is the Color Balance palette. This palette presents a series

of three sliders that control shadows, midtones, and highlights separately, each for a color complement pair. With a calibrated computer display—a critical requirement for editorial color adjustment—the corrections you see onscreen will be made to the image.

The operation of the Color Balance control is relatively simple. If the image appears to have a green color cast in the shadows, you first select Shadows and then push the slider away from Green until the image looks better. If the cast extends into the midtones, you repeat the process with the Midtones button selected. This palette works on images in any color space.

For images where a single color appears to be wrong (and the remainder of the image is fine), the Selective Color palette is a good choice for correction. This palette uses CMYK terminology but works on images in any color space. You select the target color and then adjust the "inks" that affect that color. Other colors in the image remain untouched.

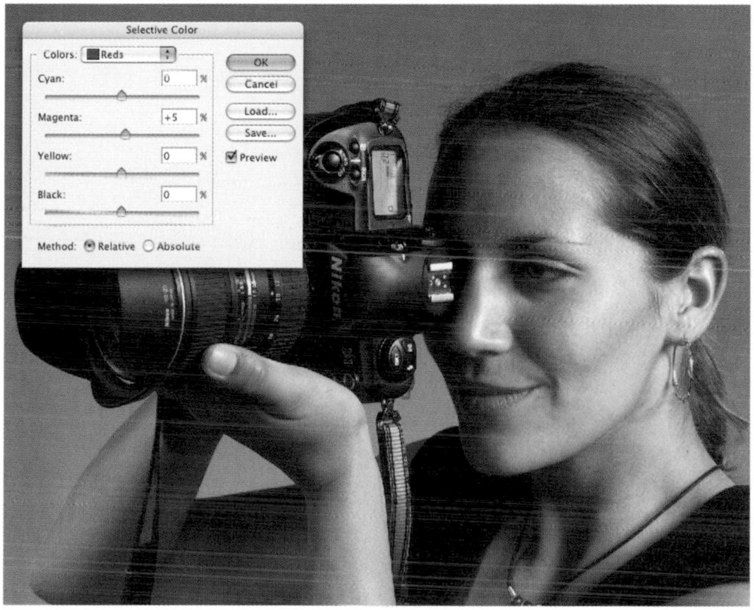

Photoshop's Selective Color palette, which operates with CMYK value sliders, works with RGB color images.

Color-correction in Photoshop (continued)

Other methods of color correction abound. Some use the Levels palette; others use the Curves palette. Others involve layers, layer masks, and combinations of the two. Consult *Real World Photoshop* from Peachpit Press or other Photoshop-specific books for more information on color correction. For more on color management, check out *Real World Color Management* from Peachpit Press.

This digital photo shows a very slight magenta cast, a result of the lighting in the studio being a little warmer than the tungsten setting on the camera. Using the Color Balance controls in Photoshop, the midtones were reduced slightly in magenta (toward green), and the highlights were reduced to a lesser degree.

The resulting image is better balanced and reflects the image qualities applied in the Color Balance palette. Most color casts are a result of the lighting in a scene being different than the camera's settings or slightly different than normal for the selected source.

Steps for preparing photos for print

1. Be sure your computer display is calibrated and your Color Settings (controlled in Adobe Bridge under Suite Color Settings) are set for your printing environment.
2. Open the image in Photoshop. If the image has an embedded color profile, use it. If it doesn't, Photoshop will ask you to assign a working space profile.

   If you know the image came from a consumer digital camera, you're safe to assign the sRGB working space.

   If the image came from a scanner or a professional digital camera, it may have a larger potential color space. Try Adobe RGB (1998) first; if the image looks good, it's OK to continue. If the image has a red or pink color cast, close the image and reopen it using the sRGB or Apple RGB working space. These smaller color spaces won't distort the color of the image by extending its red, green and blue aim points.

This image was made on a professional digital camera whose color space setting was set in-camera to Adobe RGB (1998). Opening it into that same working space in Photoshop causes the image to have normal color qualities.

Steps for preparing photos for print (continued)

3. Using the Levels control, look at the histogram and notice overall features of the tonal range. Is the range too narrow? Is the image missing black or white components? If so, move the end-point sliders in Levels to adjust the end points of the image.

   When you make these adjustments, be careful not to distort the effect the photographer wanted when taking the photo—many images are intentionally light or dark. If the photo is intentionally dark, the histogram will display this characteristic (little or no highlight).

4. You may choose to alter the image by using the Curves control in Photoshop to adjust tonality. Curves affords better control over tonal control than Levels does, because it gives you multiple control points and subtle control over different ranges of tone in the image.

5. Apply correction as needed. Useful tools for color correction include Color Balance, Curves (with individual channels selected), and Levels.

6. If appropriate, sharpen the image using the Unsharp Mask controls. Unsharp Mask creates enhanced tonal edges by creating new tones in an image at various thresholds you set in the control palette.

   Smaller images need less Unsharp Mask than larger images do. Photos of people require less sharpening than product photos do. Experiment with Unsharp Masking to develop settings that are comfortable for you and appropriate for the process you use to reproduce your images.

7. Always save your files with the color profile embedded. Doing so allows prepress workers downstream to know the boundaries of color in which you handled and edited your images. Color-managed workflows require embedded profiles to perform color conversions with the greatest color fidelity.

If an image with a large color space is imported into Photoshop with too small a working space, the colors are truncated and shift slightly toward green.

If the image is imported into Photoshop into too large a working space, the colors are again modified, this time toward red and magenta. The best practice is to open all images into a working space that is matched and appropriate to the image.

Color Terms

Additive color Color in our natural world is comprised of three primary colors: red, green, and blue. These colors behave additively, with any two creating a third, and all three creating *white*.

CMYK The usual abbreviation for cyan, magenta, yellow, and black: the inks used in color process printing.

Color filter A sheet of colored glass, plastic, or gelatin with biased transparency. A red filter, for example, allows only red light to pass through, while it absorbs light of other wavelengths. Filters are basic to color scanning and color-separation photography.

Color management Color management is the process of measuring the actual performance of a device, comparing that to a set of known color values, and making adjustments to overcome the differences. Color management is an integral part of publishing systems.

Color-matching system A system of color samples that allows a designer to specify exact colors by number or letter.

Color profile A component of a color management system, the profile describes the color behavior of a device such as a computer display, a scanner, a proof printer, or a press.

Color separation Separating a multicolor image into four monochrome components, one for each of the process colors.

Color sequence The order in which process colors are printed. A common color sequence is black-cyan-magenta-yellow. Printer's ink is formulated for a specific sequence.

Color space The color environment in which an image exists. Common color spaces include RGB (red, green, blue), CMYK (cyan, magenta, yellow, black), Lab (based on one channel for luminance and two color channels), and grayscale.

Color value The tonal value of a color, analogous to gray level on a scale from dark to light.

Duotone A duotone is a photograph printed with two colors of ink. Usually the two inks are assigned to different tonal ranges of the image.

Gray-component replacement (GCR) A method for replacing neutral grays made up of combinations of cyan, magenta, and yellow with a similar *value* of black ink. GCR improves the printability of a job by making neutral grays easier to balance on press.

High-fidelity color Any project that is printed with more than the traditional four process colors can be said to be *high fidelity color.* Most commonly this is CMYK, plus orange and green, the system developed by Pantone, Inc., called Hexachrome.

ICC The International Color Consortium, a group who establishes methods and standards for color management systems, color profiling, and the application of color in graphic arts.

JPEG An acronym for the *Joint Photographic Experts Group,* and a format for compressing still images by image analysis and modification. JPEG is a *lossy* method of compression, in that color or detail can be discarded in order to make the file smaller.

Monotone An image made with one color of ink.

Primary colors There are two systems of color that affect the graphic arts. Additive color is the color of light, made-up of red, green, and blue *primaries,* and subtractive color is the system of inks where *primaries* of cyan, magenta, and yellow ink *filter* white light to impart color to it.

Process color Multicolor printing that simulates full-color imagery. Typical systems for printing process color include cyan, magenta, yellow and black (CMYK) and Hexachrome (CMYK plus green and orange).

Quadtone An image that uses four inks.

Raster Image An image recorded by specifying the color at each cell of a grid. An individual cell in the grid is called a pixel (short for "picture element") and the grid of pixels is called a raster. Digital cameras and scanners produce raster image files, and image-editing software supports on-screen display and modification of raster images.

Raw Raw files are images from digital cameras where information recorded by the image sensor is saved without loss or in-camera adjustments.

Secondary color Secondary colors are combinations of primary colors. Mixing yellow and cyan, for example, creates green, a secondary color in the subtractive color system.

Spot color Refers to a method of specifying and printing colors in which each color is printed with its own ink rather than by a combination of the four process colors (CMYK). The purpose of spot colors can be to simplify a color match or to expand the range of colors available in a printed project.

Subtractive color The system of color used to produce printing with layers of transparent ink. Subtractive color primaries are cyan, magenta, and yellow. When combined in pairs, they produce red, green, and blue, but when all combined, they produce a muddy-brown rather than a true black, so we supplement with a fourth color, black, to compensate for this shortcoming.

SWOP The acronym for *Specifications* [for] *Web Offset Publications,* a set of printing specifications for web-fed offset printing.

Tritone An image that uses three inks.

UCR—Undercolor Removal When color separations are made, the combination of colors might exceed the Total Ink Coverage value for a certain press and paper, so the ink will not dry. UCR compensates for the excess by removing small percentages of ink. UCR describes a typical color separation, where GCR describes a more sophisticated separation process where neutral colors are modified and substituted by black ink (see GCR).

Vector graphics Digital images determined by specified points and mathematical functions. A benefit of vector graphic over raster, or bitmapped, graphics is a smaller file size.

Working space As defined by Photoshop, the color space in which an image resides while it is open in the image-editing application. Various color spaces are available, each with its own qualities. The objective is to choose one that is large enough to accommodate any color you might want in an image.

Scanning Tips

Scanning film or prints can result in great digital images, but it must be done correctly. Use the following guidelines to ensure the best scan possible:

- Calculate the required scan resolution in advance. Anticipate future needs for enlargement, which will require a higher resolution scan.
- Sharpening or correcting color during the scan can create an irreversible path. You can usually make adjustments more effectively later by using an image-editing program that lets you see the effect of your changes before you commit to them.
- Identify the key elements, or selling points, of your image. If possible, tailor the scan so those areas reproduce optimally. For instance, if the scan is for a clothing catalog, get the clothing right even if it means compromising other aspects of the image.
- If you employ a color management system, use a scanner that embeds its ICC profile in your images to record the color space used by the scanner.
- Don't scan text or previously printed graphics unless it's your only option. The results will be better if you re-create the text in your page layout application.
- When you're scanning, keep in mind that file size grows twice as fast as scan resolution. Doubling the scan resolution means there are twice as many pixels both horizontally and vertically and thus *four times as many* overall.
- Numerous scanners on the market offer impressive image restoration features. Called *Digital ICE,* these features remove dust and scratches, restore faded emulsions, and can improve the tonality of images that appear to be unusable. Using these features can save hours of retouching and restoration work on some images.

Don't trust your monitor for correcting scans. Take an extra five minutes to compare your screen color values with the same values in a CMYK swatch book.

—Andrew Faulkner, San Francisco

Choosing a scan resolution

Use the following guidelines to choose your scan resolution:

- Because black lines on a plain background tend to show jagged edges easily, line art should be scanned at high resolution. Most experts agree that you need more than 1,000 ppi in the scan to make line art appear convincing in reproduction. A resolution of 1,200 is effective for most logos and similar artwork. To scan such artwork successfully, scan it as grayscale, and then use Photoshop's Threshold control to get the best possible image.
- If you plan to use normal halftone screening for images that will print at their original size, you can conservatively calculate scanning resolution by doubling the screen ruling you plan to use. For example, if the screen ruling will be 150 lpi, the desired scan resolution is 300 ppi. Keep in mind, however, that images scanned at high resolution require more disk storage space than images scanned at lower resolution. See the section "Oversampling" for more information.
- If you plan to resize the image, allow for this in your scanning resolution. Measure the original image, decide on the size of the final printed image, and calculate the enlargement ratio of final size to original size. Factor in the anticipated enlargement ratio so that you scan at a proportionally higher resolution. Most scanner software will make these calculations for you as you work: Enter the screen frequency and the enlargement as a percentage (or the final dimensions), and the scanner will deliver a file appropriate to the image use and size.

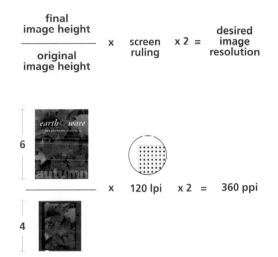

final image height / original image height x **screen ruling** x 2 = **desired image resolution**

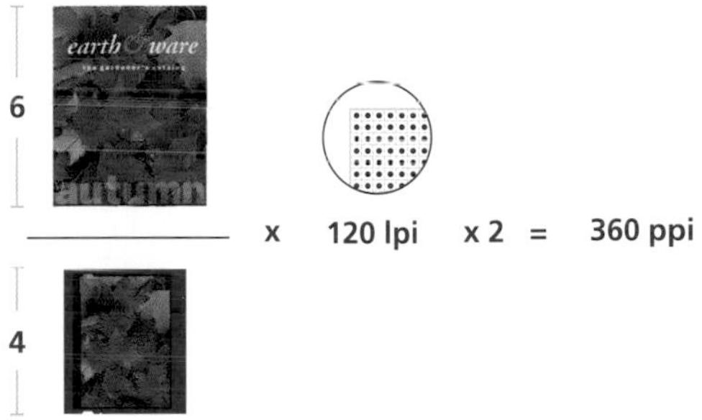

For images that will be resized, calculate the scaling factor and multiply it by twice the screen ruling.

Different scanned resolutions printed with a screen ruling of 175 lpi show that you need an adequate scan to prevent visible pixels in the final printing.

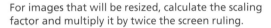

Oversampling (or overscanning)

Many images can be scanned at resolutions less than twice the output screen ruling. Images that don't contain geometric patterns, sharp edges, or straight lines can be scanned from 1.5 to 2 times the screen ruling. Fuzzy texture, foliage, and many portraits can often be scanned at even lower resolutions. In this example, even though one image has a larger file size and higher scanning resolution, the printed quality of the two images is about the same. Scanning at a higher resolution produced a larger file without improving the quality of the final image very much. The image scanned at the lower resolution requires less disk space and takes slightly less time to process while printing.

Tips for working with scanned images

- Save your scanned image in Photoshop .psd format if you work on both the Macintosh and Windows platforms and work with Adobe Creative Suite applications. InDesign and the most recent version of QuarkXPress both allow images in Photoshop format to be placed and printed directly. This eliminates the need to make an additional copy of your images for the printed publication.
- If you're using professionally scanned images, make sure you discuss your expectations with the vendor before the scanning is done. Most flaws in originals can be eliminated by a skilled scanner operator who knows what you want. Explain which images need to be especially sharp or scanned to match the original.
- To ensure good color reproduction early in the production process, you may wish to check color proofs of individual images before they are placed in a page-layout program.
- If you and your printer have determined that your images must be converted to CMYK prior to production, do that last. Smart production artists make a copy of all the images in a project and convert the images to CMYK using an appropriate ICC profile and a Photoshop Action to automate the process. Be sure to obtain a CMYK profile (or the recommendation for one) from your printer before making CMYK conversions, because these conversions are process- and paper-specific.

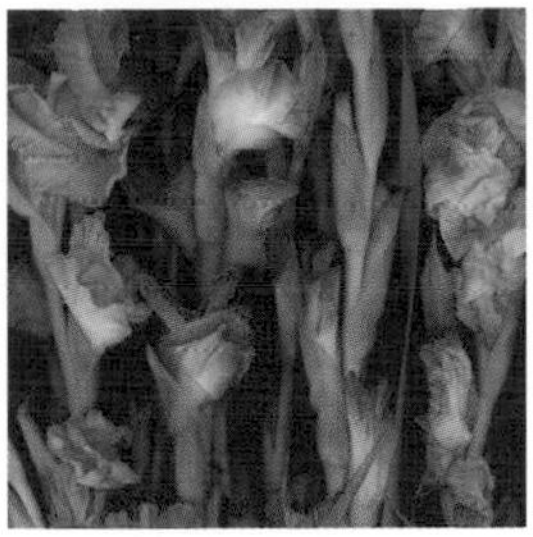

Scan resolution: 250 ppi
File size: 465K
Screen ruling: 150 lpi

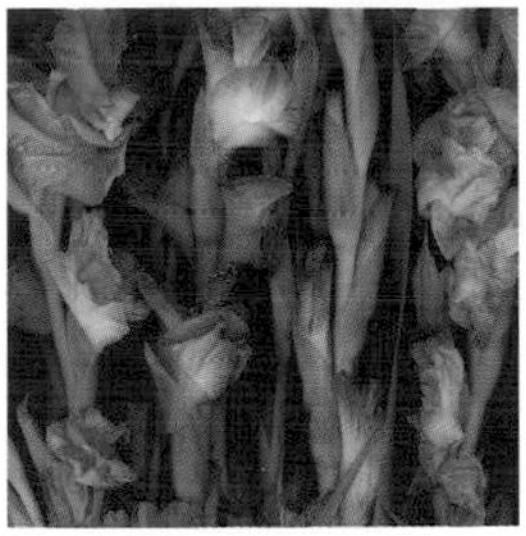

Scan resolution: 400 ppi
File size: 1165K
Screen ruling: 150 lpi

An image oversampled to a great degree prints exactly the same as an image at the correct sampling value. It takes longer to process and image in the platesetter.

Tips for working with digital camera images

- Digital photos from professional cameras contain an embedded ICC profile. Always use that profile when Photoshop asks for instructions on how to handle a profile mismatch.
- Images from nearly all consumer digital cameras are in the sRGB color space. They may not have an embedded ICC profile when you open them. If you assign this profile while opening digital camera images in Photoshop, you'll almost always see pleasing—and reasonably accurate—color.
- Digital camera images have a fixed resolution that's set in the camera (or defined by the camera's image sensor). Amateur photographers often lower the resolution of their camera to fit more photos on their memory card. When you open these files, you may discover that they can't be reproduced at adequate size. To check or set the resolution of any digital image, use Photoshop's Image > Image Size palette. With the Resample Image checkbox not selected, you can enter resolution values needed for print and see the impact of resolution on reproduction size.
- Most digital cameras are good at defining the white balance of an image at the time it's exposed. If the image doesn't look good, however, it's reasonably easy to correct for white balance problems. Use the Photoshop Image > Adjustments > Photo Filter palette, where you can assign common filters to correct for simple lighting errors.
- When you're working with professional digital cameras, it's always smart to use the raw file format (built into the camera) and then open those images with the Camera Raw plug-in in Photoshop. Raw conversions allow for image interpolation, *subsampling* (increasing and decreasing the image resolution), and color correction, among other controls, at the time the image is opened.

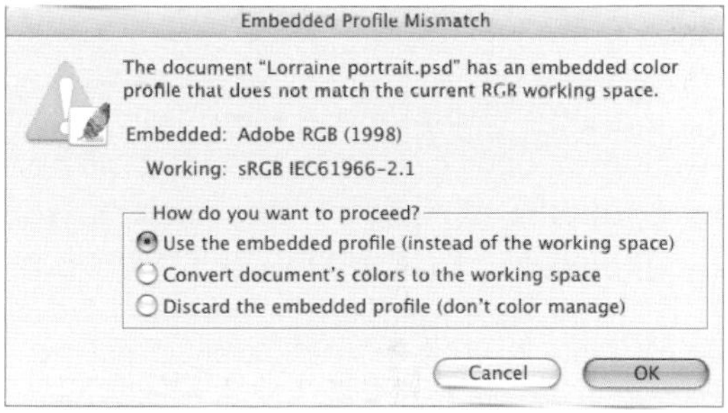

When you're presented with the Embedded Profile Mismatch dialog in Photoshop, it's best to use the embedded profile (if present); it represents a measure of the image as the photographer created it.

You can manipulate raw images using Photoshop's Camera Raw plug-in. There are controls for resolution, color temperature, tint, sharpness, and more. This palette only works on images saved by cameras in their raw format.

Multitone printing

A single plate on a printing press can reproduce a nice tonal range, but the density of the ink seldom makes a print that rivals a real photograph. Multitone printing with gray or other inks has been used for years to enrich the tonal range when printing black-and-white photographs.

Duotones, *tritones*, and *quadtones* are grayscale images printed with two, three, or four inks, respectively. The process is similar to process color separation printing, but the plates deliver one or more spot color inks instead of—or in addition to—the process colors. Duotone, tritone, and quadtone printing can dramatically improve the overall appearance of images.

You can create duotones, tritones, and quadtones in Photoshop (Image > Mode > Duotone). Doing so lets you decide how tonal levels in the original should be translated into percentages of the separate inks in print. To create a duotone in Photoshop, you specify tonal curves (one for each ink) that control how gray levels in the original are to be converted into halftone dot size. Some duotone settings are provided in Photoshop, but you can also create curves for colors other than those provided.

This monochrome image, produced with a single color of ink, looks good, but adding a second or third color can enhance it even more. With cyan, magenta, and yellow at your disposal, you can create duotones from monochromatic images so they take on the tint of the desired color ink or just enrich the tonality of the image. The possibilities are endless. To the right are three examples of simple duotone modifications you can easily make to an image.

By adding cyan, magenta, or yellow ink to the grayscale image and favoring the added color in the duotone curves, the image assumes a tint and has greater density. Subtle variations in the curves can make the color relationship change considerably.

Multitone printing (continued)

Duotone images printed in a publication with just two colors of ink can look as rich as full-color photographs if the curves are set to emphasize the qualities of the images and the spot colors chosen.

As a general rule, one color (typically the darker) is used to render the full tonality of the image, often with the midtones reduced in intensity to allow the second color to show. The second color is then used to tint the midtones through the shadows. If you shape the curves appropriately, the additional colors enrich the image. Adjust the curves until the characteristics of color are pleasing. Try to keep the highlights in the image untinted by the second color; doing so keeps highlights in the image convincingly light.

An alternative in duotone creation is to use the two colors in near-equal amounts that more simply tint the photo with the second color. Doing so doubles the density of ink printed and makes the image look richer in print. The tint of the second color is less evident using this technique.

You can create handsome sepia-tone images from monochrome images printed with three or four colors of ink. These duotones can be used to make grayscale images look antique, and the result is much nicer than printing the same images with black only.

There is no reason that duotones must use spot color inks; they can just as easily be constructed from any of the four process color inks with great results.

When you've created a duotone setting that you like, you can save it from the Duotone palette and apply it to other images. You can also convert duotones into RGB images or CMYK images (Image > Mode > RGB) to take advantage of a tonal property you've created in the duotone environment.

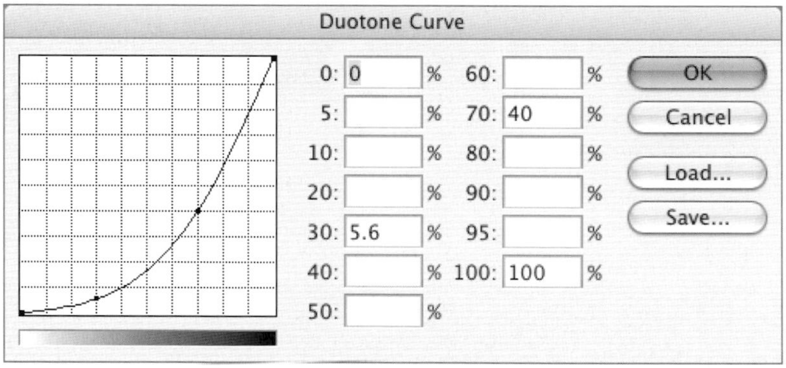

The Photoshop Duotone Curve dialog box allows you to specify the distribution of each ink by specifying a dot percentage for each color on a curve. In this example, a cyan-black duotone has been created. The black carries the entire image with midtones reduced in tonality, whereas the cyan color is allowed to tint the image significantly.

Image Size, Interpolation, and Resampling

A digital image contains a fixed number of pixels, and the dimensions at which it will be printed define its resolution (or vice versa). Existing digital images can be resampled to new sizes (larger or smaller) using the Image > Image Size palette in Photoshop.

Resampling occurs when you change the number of pixels in a digital image. Resampling alters the file resolution and thus its reproduction size. Resampling up or down is accomplished in software by projecting an image on a new array with a different number of pixels, known as *scaling*. When an image is scaled, *interpolation* is used to construct color levels for the pixels in the new array.

Continuous-tone image

2X enlarged section using Bicubic interpolation

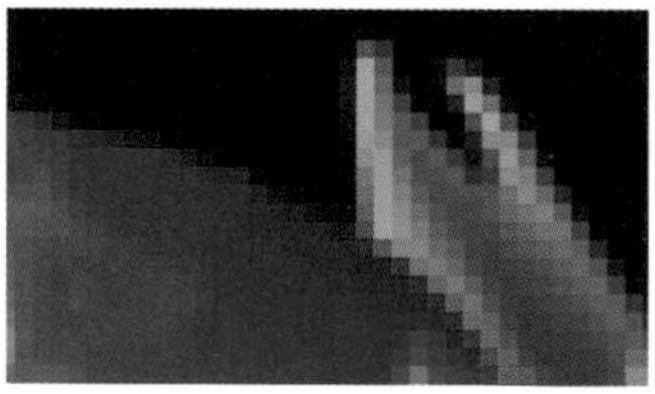

2X enlarged section using Nearest Neighbor interpolation

Grayscale image (converted using Channel Mixer in Photoshop)

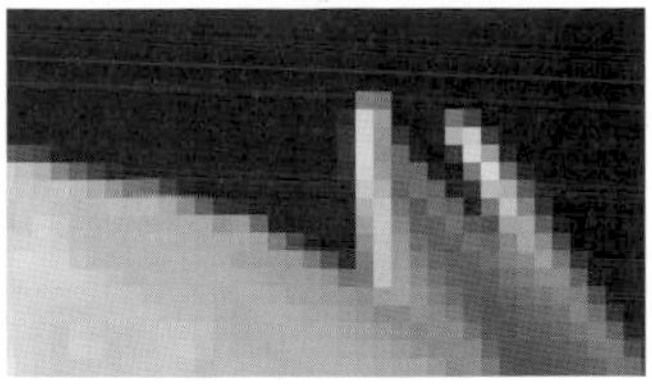

2X enlarged section using Bicubic interpolation

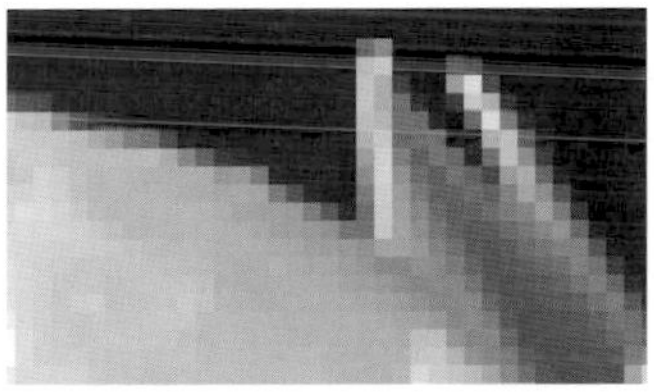

2X enlarged section using Nearest Neighbor interpolation

The image as it would appear if scanned at a low resolution or interpolated too much. When pixels or patterns of pixels become visible, the image has been enlarged too much for the current viewing distance and printing process.

Image Size, Interpolation, and Resampling (continued)

Subsampling—reducing the resolution—is occasionally done to cause the image to go through a prepress system more efficiently.

Here are some things to remember about scaling and resampling digital images:

- In general, it's best to scan an image at the scale and resolution you need it, to avoid having either to resample or to resize the image later. With images from professional digital cameras, it's easy to open them at one of a variety of sizes using the Camera Raw palette.
- You can increase the resolution of a digital image by fitting it into a smaller space. Doing that doesn't involve any change in the size of the file and doesn't require resampling. The result may be an image that has higher resolution, but it doesn't appear any better in print.
- Subsampling works best if you divide the original resolution by a whole number factor. For instance, if your original image is 600 ppi, resample to make the new resolution a simple fraction of 600 ppi such as 300, 150, or 75 ppi.
- You can increase an image's resolution using Photoshop's Image Size palette. Experimentation with this tool will reveal the extremes to which an image can be modified without visible harm to its detail. Some imaging experts assert that it's best to interpolate images to higher resolutions by even factors—doubling the size exactly, for example. Others claim the best results when they make several steps upward—such as 20 percent increments applied several times.
- Using the Unsharp Mask filter in Photoshop can compensate for some of the blurring introduced by resampling.
- Once an image is resampled, the original information can't be recovered except by rescanning it or reopening it from the digital camera (although you can step backward in the History palette if the file is still open).

200-ppi scan resolution; 869K file size.
No sharpening has been applied.

100-ppi scan resolution; 386K file size. Unsharp Mask has been applied, proving that with some images, a smaller file size combined with a bit of sharpening makes the image reproducible.

Graphic File Formats

The file format you choose for your graphics depends on your workflow and final output.

Both InDesign and QuarkXPress now support native Photoshop documents, complete with image layers and effects. InDesign also lets you place native Illustrator files into a page layout document. To reduce the number of document versions, and to see the best quality image onscreen, use native Photoshop files in either page layout application. Use Illustrator files in InDesign and Illustrator EPS files in the latest versions of QuarkXPress.

For duotones (and tritones and quadtones), use the EPS format. But don't use EPS for other raster images (photographs). The EPS format doesn't support some of the embedded information needed by the latest versions of InDesign and QuarkXPress.

The TIFF file format is useful for grayscale or color images. TIFF supports layers, clipping paths, and most color spaces. It also allows ICC color profiles to be embedded, which makes this file format a good choice for page layouts.

Desktop Color Separation (DCS) files are EPS files that combine a low-resolution display image with high-resolution data for color separations. DCS supports additional colors beyond CMYK. Up to 24 channels can be saved in a DCS file, those colors created in Photoshop's Multichannel mode. In the page layout application, each color in a DCS image is treated as a spot color.

Photo CD files contain raster images in several resolutions and are stored on a special CD in a format called YCC. Photo CD files can store images from 35mm, 70mm, 120mm, and 4-by-5-inch film. Although it's possible to get film scanned and stored on Photo CD discs, such discs aren't common today.

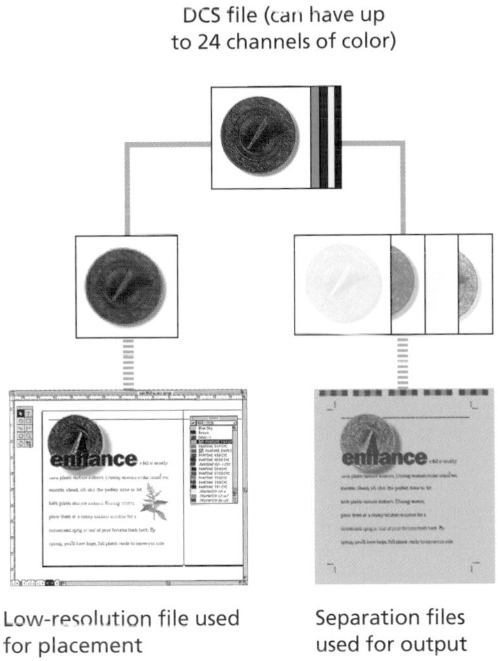
DCS file (can have up
to 24 channels of color)
Low-resolution file used
for placement
Separation files
used for output

Open Prepress Interface

Open Prepress Interface (OPI) is a method of using low-resolution images in a page layout and then substituting high-resolution images at the time of printing. The process is sometimes known by the term Automatic Picture Replacement (APR); both terms are trademarks of the companies that developed them.

When you use an application that supports OPI, your service provider can scan your artwork, keep the high-resolution images, and give you low-resolution placeholder images to use in design and layout. You don't need the large storage capacity or fast processing speed required to store high-resolution images.

After you create your publication using a page-layout program that supports OPI, you or your service provider can generate a PostScript file containing OPI comments that specify the page, placement, size, and cropping of any TIFF images. Your prepress service provider uses a prepress application that automatically substitutes the high-resolution versions of the images while imaging.

If you intend to edit your images, you must use the high-resolution images; low-resolution images are *for position, scaling, and cropping only.*

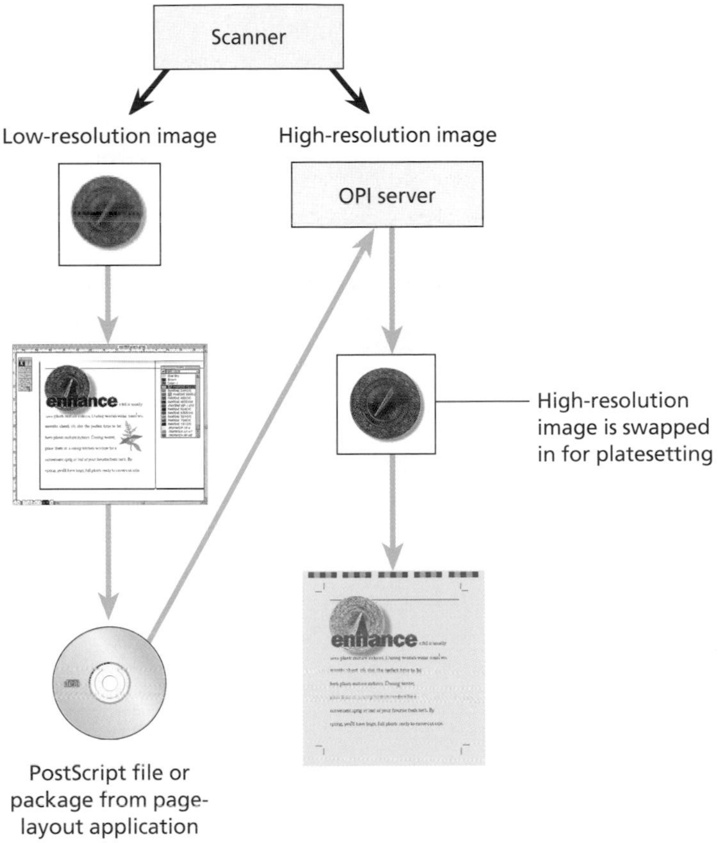

Low-resolution file used for placement in the page layout

High-resolution file substituted for separations

Special Techniques

Bleeds

Printing an object to the edge of the final printed piece requires creating a *bleed*. A bleed extends objects off the print area to ensure that when the paper is trimmed during the finishing process, the ink coverage extends to the edge of the paper.

The convention for bleeds is to extend the image .125 inch off the sheet. It's important to remember that the image will be trimmed: Don't put any important information at the edge that is needed in the image at or close to the bleed line.

Bleeds extend to the edge of the paper.

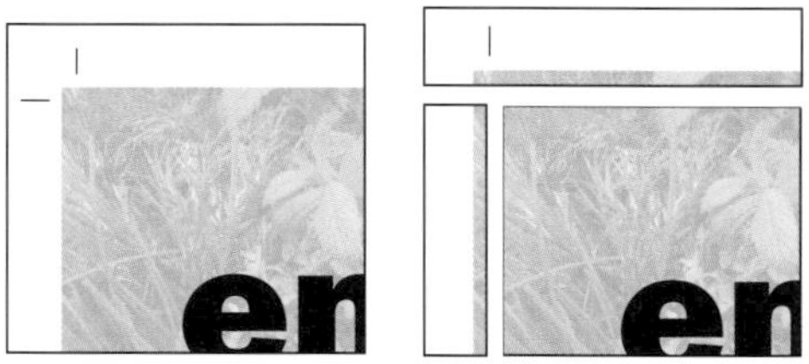

Trim marks indicate where the page will be cut.

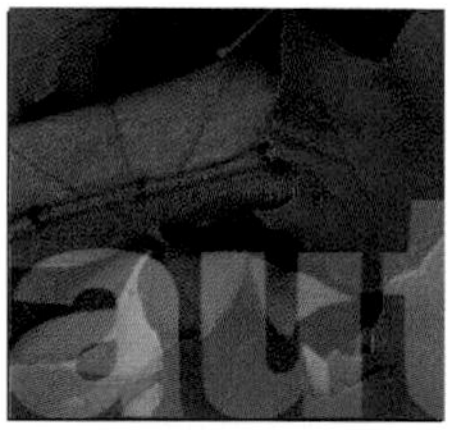

Avoid aligning objects exactly with the edge of the page.

Adjust the design so trimming looks intentional.

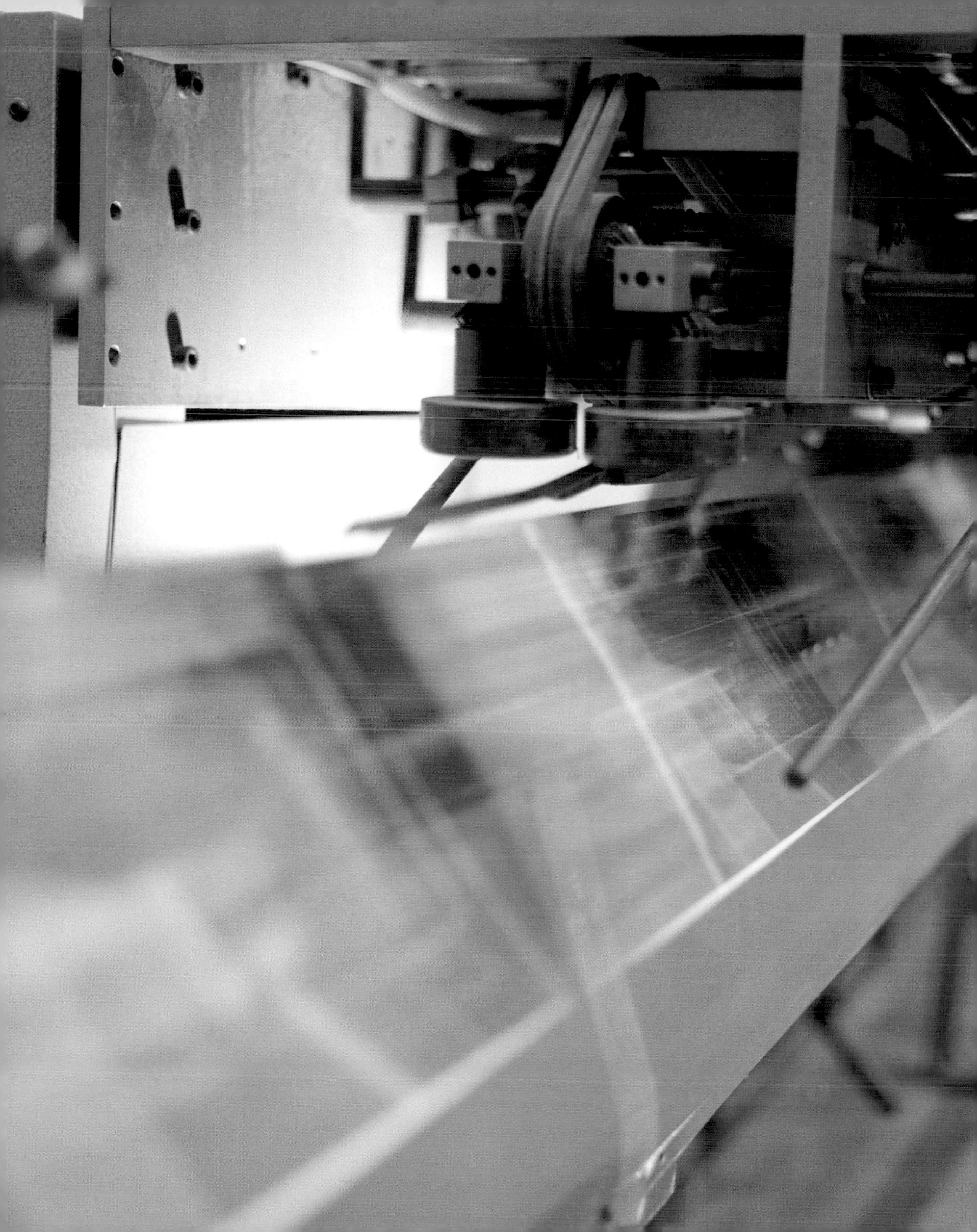

Crossovers

A *crossover* is a printed object that extends from one page to the next. Because a single object is printed on two sheets of paper (or on two sides of the same sheet of paper), the pages must be carefully aligned in the final printed piece.

Binding methods affect crossover position and alignment. An object that spans the gutter may seem to disappear when the pages are bound, so you need to adjust the design accordingly. Also, when pages are gathered together for binding, some of the pages can be pushed out slightly. This phenomenon, called *creep,* can cause gaps or misalignment between the two parts of the crossover.

Follow these guidelines when creating a crossover:

- Avoid printing important text across two pages, because part of it will be lost in the binding. Some designers add a small amount of space to headlines that pass through the fold of a crossover so the text will be legible.
- Diagonal artwork in crossovers can exaggerate misalignment in folding and binding. Consider how an image will look if part of it is removed in the binding process. Adding an artificial extension in the artwork can partially compensate for the effects of binding.
- Color can print differently on opposite sides of the paper. This may be due to the paper surface's qualities or to printing conditions. A crossover can often fall between different sides or different sheets of paper, and this can exaggerate color differences in two-page spreads.

To reduce the impact of differences in the appearance of color in crossovers, consider printing with a spot color those colors which are significant in the design and which must cross over from front to back of the sheet, or from one sheet to another.

Crossovers extend from one page to another.

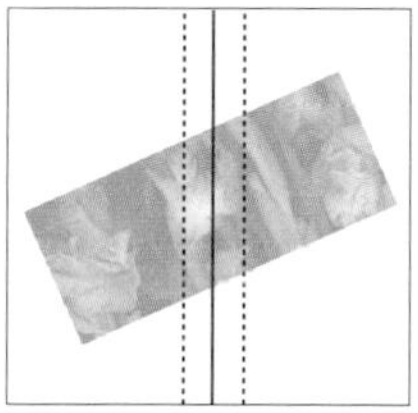

Before binding

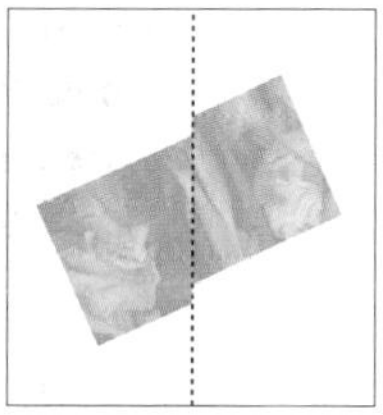

After binding

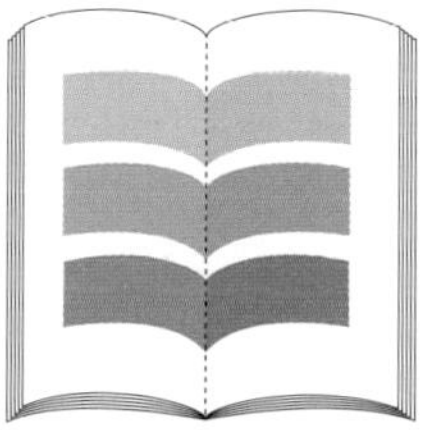

Color shifts can occur when crossovers print on different forms.

Thicker rules help conceal misalignment.

Overprinting and preview

Overprinting can be used to create additional colors and special effects. Normally, when you produce a document with overlapping objects, the top object replaces, or *knocks out*, the colors beneath it. Overprinting prints the colors on top of each other.

Overprinting colors with different inks combines the ink values in the overprinted color. For example, if a background color contains 50% C and the overprinted color has 60% M, the overprinted area consists of 50% C and 60% M.

When you overprint colors with components of the same ink, the combined color assumes the percentage value of the topmost item (and never more than 100% of any color). For example, if a background color contains 50% C, and the overprinted color contains 20% C and 60% M, the printed color where the colors overlap contains 20% C and 60% M.

Overprinting can also be used to specify varnishes in some graphic elements. Specifying a varnish as a spot color and then declaring that spot color to overprint causes the plate for the spot color to have an image of the overprint. Though this technique works with text and some graphics, it doesn't work with placed images.

Overprinting can cause problems on the press; be sure to talk with your commercial printer about their limits for total ink coverage, and be sure not to exceed the value they recommend (typically 250–320%) in any combination of overprinted inks.

Also, never use the color registration on any artwork or text in your project. The registration color—defined as 100% of every color printed—is only for printer's marks used to control register on press.

Overprinting can create a new color.

Overprinting can change the look of a color unexpectedly.

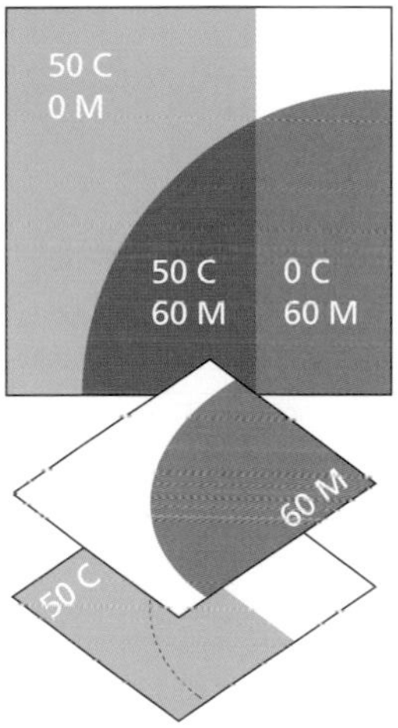

Overprinting objects without common inks combines the ink values where the objects overlap.

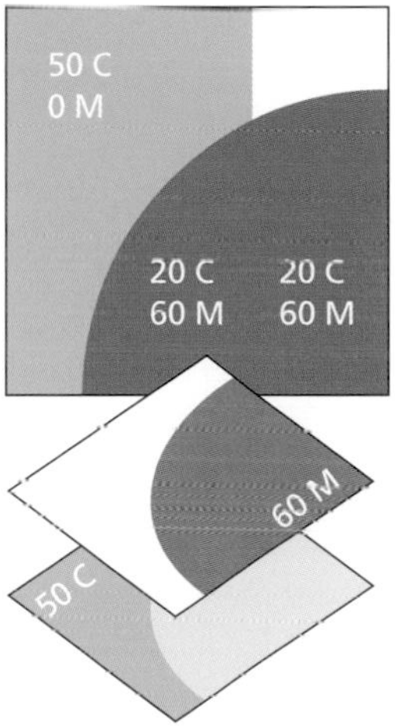

Overprinting objects with common inks reveals the topmost of the overprinted ink colors of the common colors. Different colors overprint as a combination of the values of the colors.

Compensating for Register Error

When you examine printed work, you'll often notice register problems in areas where colors meet. These are usually caused by the paper stretching or shifting slightly on the printing press. Where inks print out of register, gaps or color shifts appear between the objects. Gaps are especially likely when adjacent objects share no common color and when objects knock out rather than overprint. Overprinting is often used as a way to reduce the effects of press register error. Another way of hiding flaws in register involves expanding one region into another by adding a border stroke called a *trap*.

Trapping

Some prepress systems provide automated trapping of artwork as a process step in file preparation for platesetting. This method of trapping is by far the best because the trap elements, their color, and their values are determined by sophisticated software algorithms. If trapping is available from your prepress provider, take advantage of that service.

Manual trapping requires a thorough knowledge of color and design and of when trapping is likely to be necessary. A publication designed with several interacting spot colors requires trapping because the colors don't share a common ink. A publication containing several process colors without common colors may also require trapping.

On the other hand, not all printing requires trapping. Designs that contain isolated areas of solid color don't need to be trapped because there are no adjacent colors that could show gaps if register errors occur. Designs composed of process colors where adjacent areas share sufficient percentages of component inks don't require trapping, because misregister would reveal the common inks instead of leaving a gap. Photographs don't need to be trapped because the distribution of colors in a typical scene provides enough randomness to prevent large areas of a single color from existing adjacent to large areas of a different color.

An effective trap should compensate for misregister without distorting the shapes of the objects on the page. If trapping results in visible distortion, it may be preferable to protect against register error by overprinting all or part of an object. Overprinting black lines and black text can help to avoid the problem, even when these objects appear on a colored background. Illustrations that make extensive use of black outlines, such as cartoons or certain highly stylized art, require little or no trapping.

Page designed to avoid trapping

Page requiring trapping

Chokes and spreads

A *spread* traps a light foreground object to a dark background. A *choke* traps a light background to a dark foreground object. Because the darker of two adjacent colors defines the visible edge of the object or text, spreading the lighter color slightly into the darker color maintains the visual edge of the artwork.

A solid color object that overlaps both a lighter and darker background requires both spreads and chokes to be applied for effective trapping.

Trapping process colors

Process colors that share sufficient percentages of component inks don't require trapping because misregister reveals a color that has a component of each of the adjacent colors. In the example shown here, the first two colors share sufficient percentages of common inks that misregister reveals a color that isn't distracting. However, the second two colors require trapping because they contain ink percentages that differ enough to reveal a third color when the colors are printed out of register. When adjacent colors don't have inks in common, a trap is required.

Items reversed-out of a rich black (black plus a percentage of one or more other colors) require a trapping technique called a *keep-away trap*. When you trap such items, the under-printed colors are made slightly smaller than the black area so that press register error doesn't result in a tiny fringe of color. Should the press go out of register, the underprinting colors are covered by the black area.

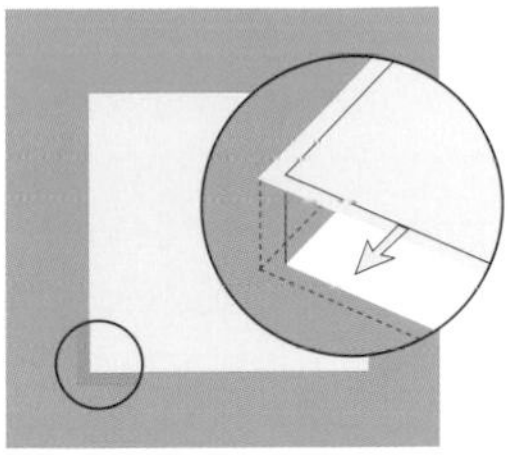

Spread

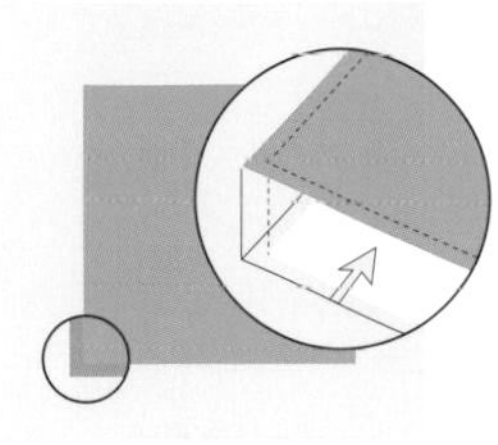

Choke

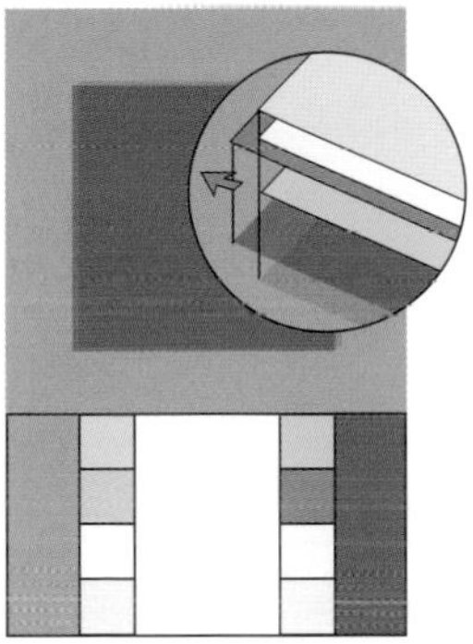

These colors share sufficient percentages of component inks that poor press register reveals common inks.

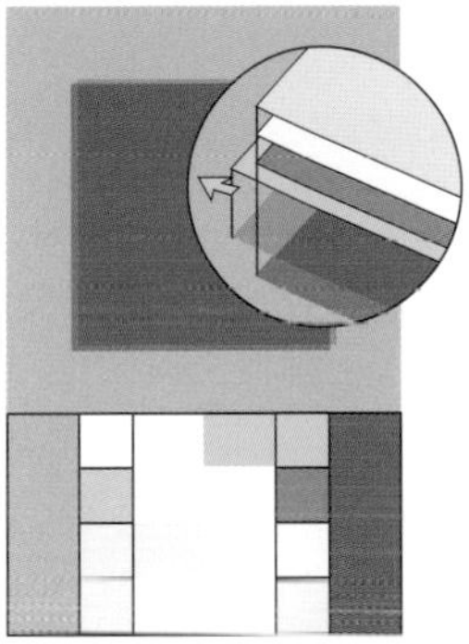

These colors don't share sufficient percentages of component inks, so poor register reveals a noticeable third color.

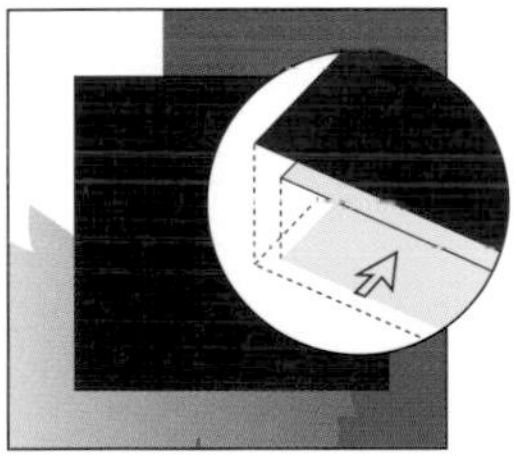

The nonblack color of a rich black is pulled away from the edge…

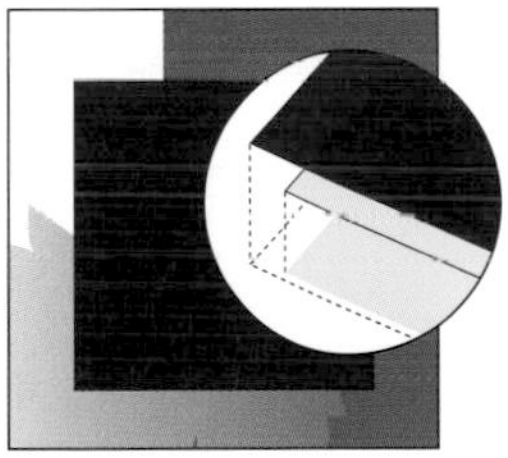

so that when register error occurs, the under-printing color won't show.

Overprinting to cover register error

In some situations, overprinting text and objects can be preferable to trapping as a way to hide register error. For example, small text and hairlines are distorted by trapping (the trapping strokes that are added fatten the thin lines). Overprinting preserves the shape of the object and the legibility of the text.

Before you overprint fine text or thin lines, evaluate whether misregister will be more noticeable than a possible variation in the line or text color. Keep in mind that your solution should provide the least distraction between text (or line) and background, should a register error occur. Ask these questions to evaluate your situation:

- If gaps appear due to register error, will they be noticeable?
- Will the text change to an undesirable color if it's overprinted on the background?
- Will trapping distort the text characters?

Printing black trapping lines around images is a common use of overprinting to prevent register error from showing. This is the technique used for decades to print comic book art. All drawing elements are surrounded by a black outline that is set to overprint. The overprinted line can hide most register error. The line thickness is typically set to one-half the halftone screen frequency (.003 inch for a 150 lines per inch [lpi] project). This technique doesn't lend itself to many styles of illustration artwork, but it works well when it's used appropriately.

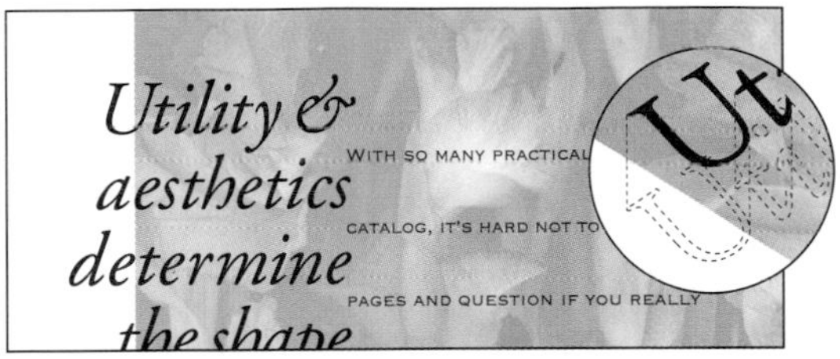

Overprinted black text

Overprinted trap line

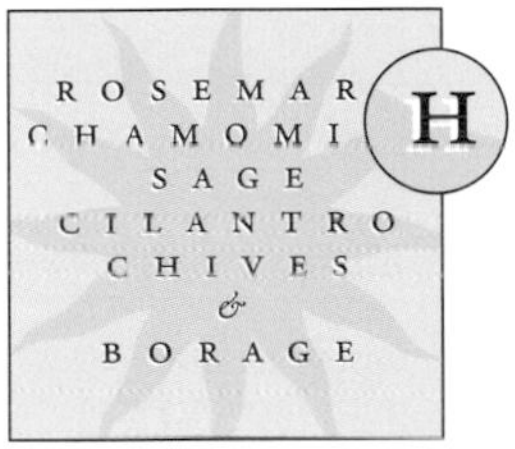

Black text set to knock out, out of register

Black text set to overprint, out of register

Trapping methods

Overprinting colors with inks in common

If objects share common ink colors, it is not necessary to trap the colors. In this case, the common ink hides slight areas of misregistration.

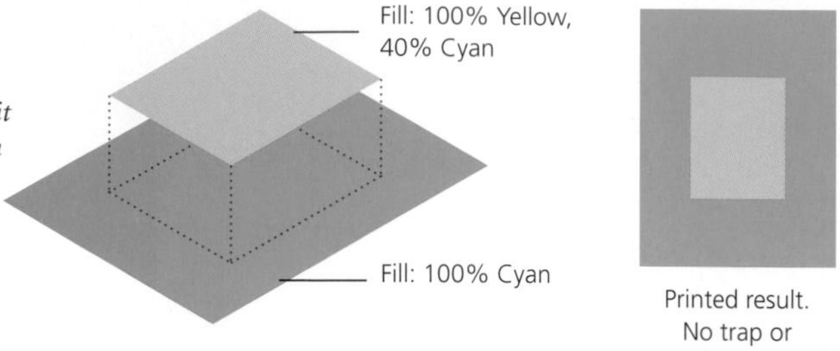

Overprinting colors with no inks in common

If objects do not share common ink colors, use trap to add the overprint color to the background color where the two overlap.

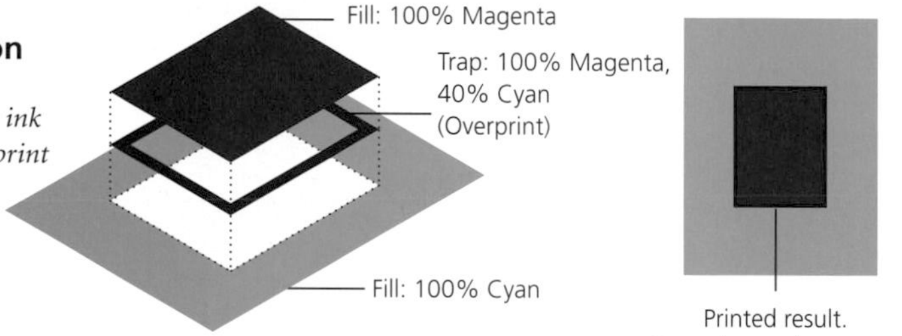

Trapping lines

Use when printing lines on a colored or black background.

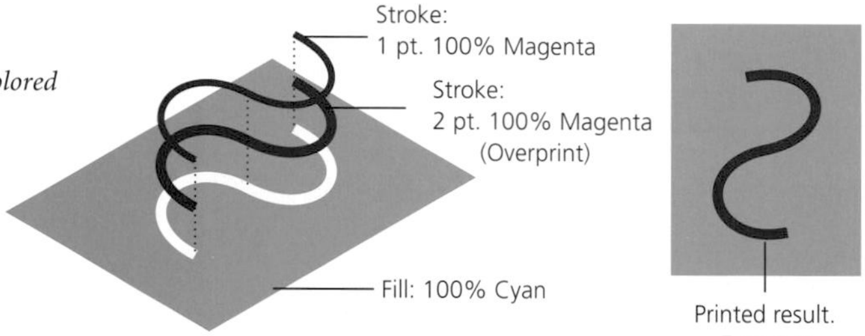

Black lines overprint (rich black background)

Use when your illustration or type is reversed-out of a rich black background.

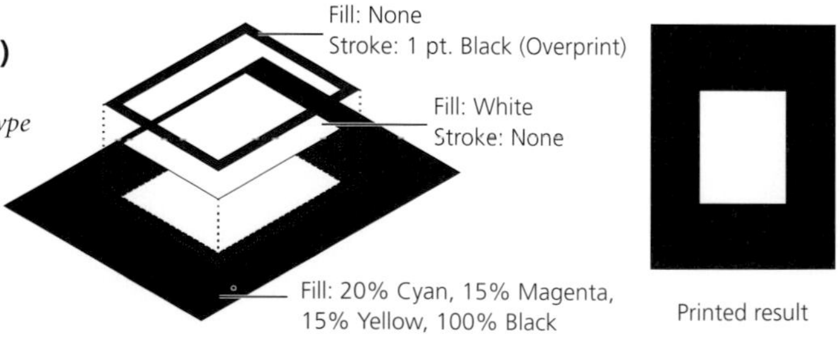

Butt-fit

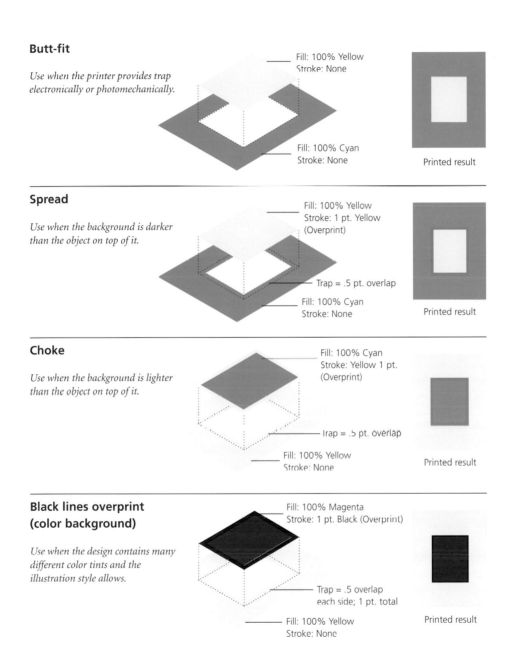

Use when the printer provides trap electronically or photomechanically.

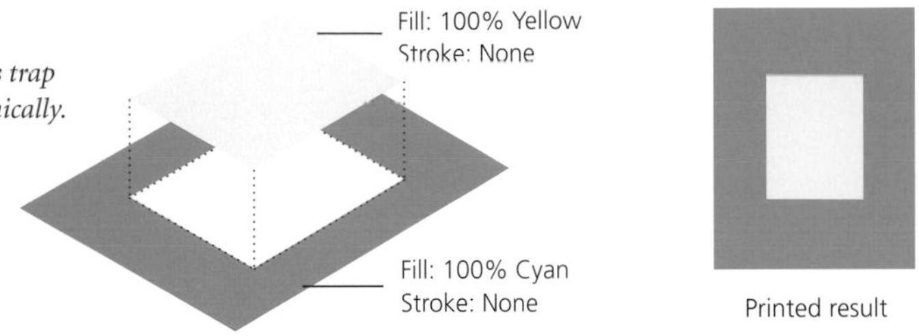

Spread

Use when the background is darker than the object on top of it.

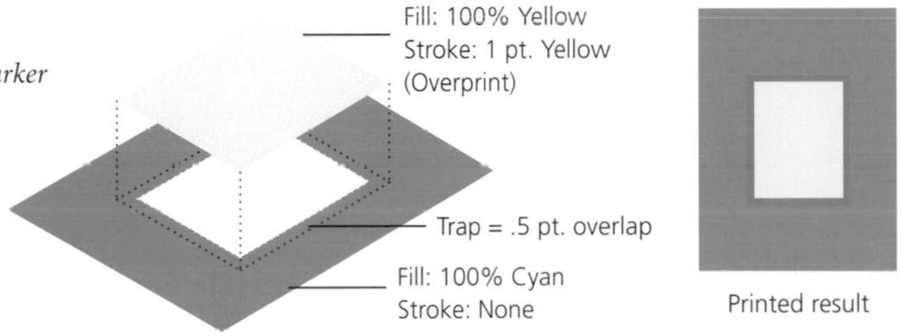

Choke

Use when the background is lighter than the object on top of it.

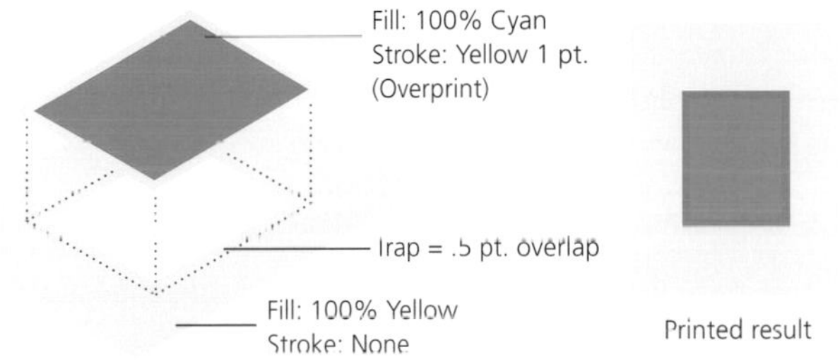

Black lines overprint (color background)

Use when the design contains many different color tints and the illustration style allows.

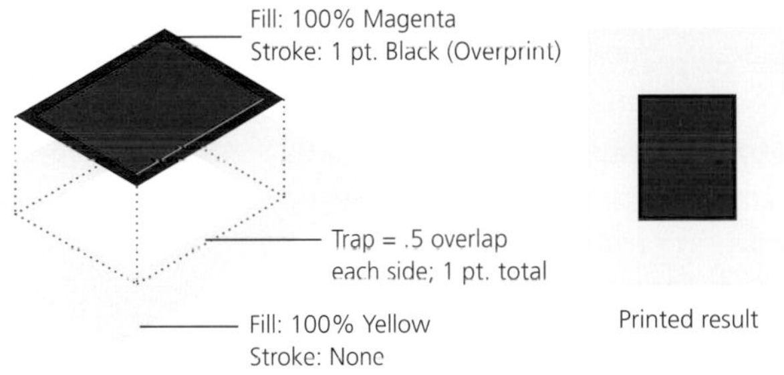

Screen Frequency, Resolution, and Gray Levels

Screen frequency, also called *screen ruling* or *halftone frequency*, refers to the number of lines per inch (lpi) of halftone dots in the finished printing. The relationship between the platesetter resolution (dpi) and the screen ruling (lpi) determines the halftone quality of the printed output. The same two factors also affect the number of gray levels or color tones available, measures of the *tonal depth* in the halftone image.

The screen ruling used for a job depends on the resolution of the platesetter as well as the paper stock and type of press used to print the publication. Common screen frequencies are used for most printing processes; these are defined in part by industry quality standards and traditions.

Full-color newspapers are commonly printed using a screen ruling of 100 lpi because newsprint absorbs a great deal of ink and the presses operate at high speed. A higher screen frequency would oversaturate the newsprint and make the images look muddy. Full-color magazines on coated paper are usually printed with a screen ruling of 133 lpi, whereas sheet-fed and commercial printing is typically done at 150 lpi. Garment printing created with the screen-printing process generally uses a halftone frequency of 50–65 lpi.

Halftone screen frequency also determines the size of a halftone *cell*, which in turn dictates the minimum size of a halftone *dot* (highest frequency). The halftone dot is made up of printer dots (measured in dpi); printer (imagesetter or platesetter) resolution determines the number of dots available to create the halftone dot. The relationship between screen ruling and printer resolution determines the number of gray steps that can be simulated. As the screen ruling increases, the size of the halftone cell decreases; fewer printer dots are available to create the halftone dot, so fewer gradations can be represented and the image may lose depth.

To calculate how many levels of gray are available at a particular screen ruling and output resolution, use the formula shown in the accompanying chart. Most output devices produce 256 gray steps (for photographic images). This is a process limitation of PostScript. PostScript platesetters draw algorithmic gradations (those created in Illustrator, for example) using a different process and aren't limited to 256 steps.

Every platesetter available today (and most film imagesetters) have adequate machine resolution to generate 150 lpi halftones—or finer—without tonal degradation.

imagesetter or platesetter resolution	maximum line screen for 256 gray steps
300	19
400	25
600	38
900	56
1000	63
1270	79
1446	90
1524	95
1693	106
2000	125
2400	150
2540	159
3000	188
3252	203
3600	225
4000	250

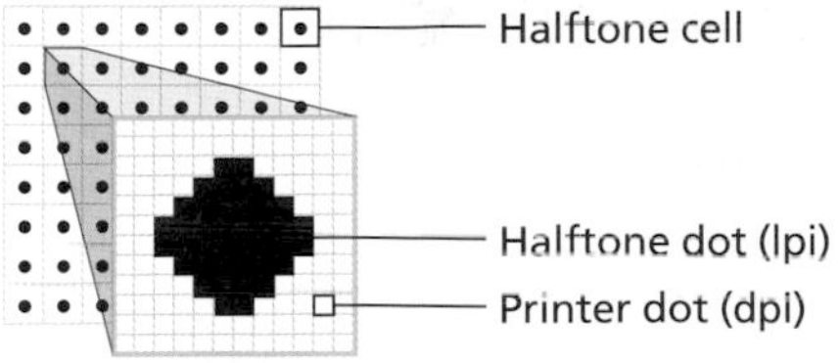

High-resolution imaging devices, such as computer-to-plate (CTP) systems, have enough machine resolution to draw halftone dots with full tonality. Low-resolution devices, such as laser printers, don't have the resolution to draw halftone images with as many gray steps between black and white.

(machine resolution ÷ screen ruling)^2 + 1 = potential shades of gray

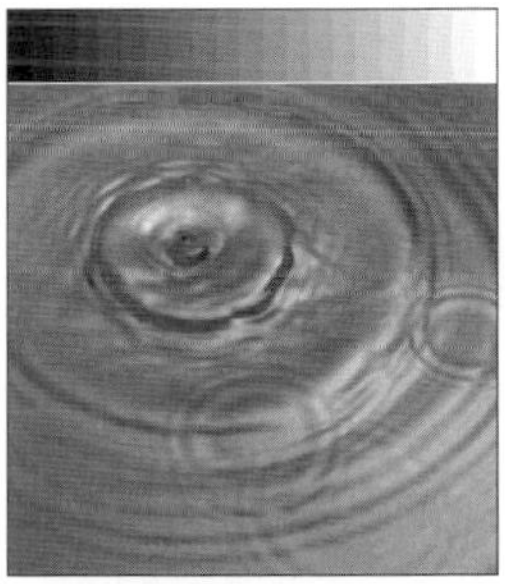

Laser printer: (600 dpi ÷ 60 lpi)^2 + 1 = 101 shades of gray

The laser printer can print black and white, but it doesn't have adequate machine resolution to draw many steps of gray in between (the problem is exaggerated for this illustration).

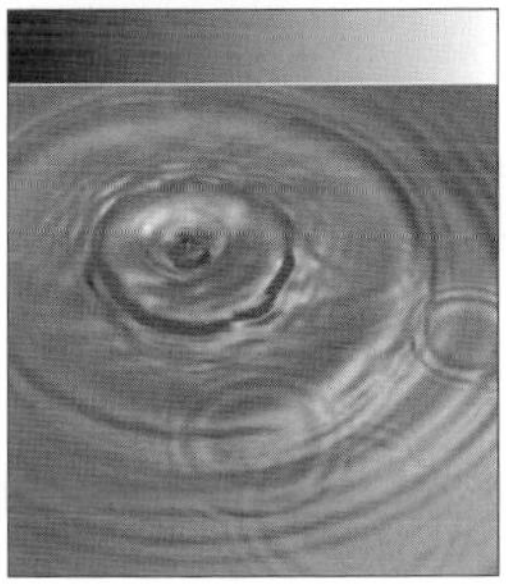

Platesetter: (3600 dpi ÷ 175 lpi)^2 + 1 = 577 shades of gray

The platesetter has enough resolution to draw full tonality at most common screen rulings. PostScript has a 256-tone limit for photographic grayscales, so the image would be limited to 256 gray values despite the theoretical 577 shown here.

Dot Gain

Continuous-tone images are reproduced with halftone dots of different sizes—large dots reproduce dark tones and small dots reproduce light tones. During the reproduction process, the dots change in size, becoming larger. This phenomenon is called *dot gain.*

There are several sources of dot gain, all of which are highly predictable. Dot gain occurs when the plate cylinder transfers its image to the blanket cylinder on press. Additional gain occurs when the dot is transferred to the paper—the pressure of the press forces some ink into the paper, which causes the inked halftone dots to spread very slightly. Uncoated papers cause more gain than coated papers do.

The amount of dot gain for a particular press and paper depends on the printing environment and the halftone frequency (higher line screens cause greater dot gain). Individual dot gain depends primarily on the size of the dot. The midtone (50 percent) dot has the greatest circumference, so it increases the most. Small highlight dots and shadow dots show little gain (they are actually small white dots in the center of black halftone cells). The accompanying graph shows the typical dot gain from file to press-sheet stage plotted against the percentage dot value (representing tone) in the original. The curve peaks at the 50 percent tonal value and approaches zero at both ends.

Halftone-dot percentages are measured with a *densitometer*—an instrument used for measuring the density of ink on printed substrates. A dot-gain value refers to what happens to midtone dots as a percentage of change in area. A 20 percent dot gain (typical for offset printing on gloss papers) means that the 50 percent dot will print on paper at 70 percent.

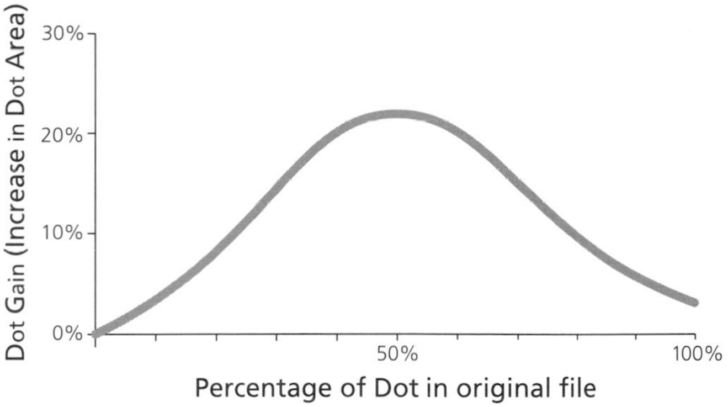

Typical dot gain for sheet-fed offset printing on coated paper at 150 lpi. Uncoated papers show significantly greater amounts of gain.

Normal tonal reproduction of an image results in predictable dot gain.

Excessive dot gain makes the midtones in an image appear dark and makes the image muddy. Photoshop displays images with standard dot gain to simulate the appearance of the image as it will print. Printing color images with ICC profile conversions also compensates for measured dot gain.

Paper quality and dot gain

Papers and coatings come in a large variety of types and are intended for many different purposes:

- **Newsprint.** A coarser paper made mostly from wood pulp and that is highly porous. It's manufactured almost exclusively for printing newspapers. The dot gain for newsprint is typically 30 percent or more. Common halftone screen frequencies used for newspaper printing are 85 lpi and 100 lpi.
- **Uncoated paper.** Any number of different types of paper that aren't coated with a gloss surface treatment. Dot gain for uncoated paper is roughly 25 percent. On web-fed offset presses, uncoated papers are usually printed at 133 lpi; sheet-fed presses use 150–175 lpi.
- **Coated paper.** Paper that has been given a shiny coating in manufacture, helping to seal the paper and reduce dot gain. On a sheet-fed press, the dot gain on coated stock can be as low as 15 percent, although 20 percent is more typical. High-quality grayscale and four-color images are usually printed on coated papers because such papers reflect more light and have a greater measured and visible gamut of colors available.

- **Calendered paper.** Paper that has had a normal finishing step applied that involves heat and pressure. Calendering freshly made paper is analogous to ironing cloth. Calendering is used on some papers in order to get a smoother, less porous surface. Calendered stock has dot gain that is slightly better than that of uncoated stock, typically between 20 to 25 percent, compared to 25 to 30 percent for uncoated stock.

When you're using a color-managed workflow, the ICC color profiles applied to images and documents as they are processed compensate for dot gain.

Linked Graphics, Package, and Prepare for Output

When you place a photo or illustration in a page layout, the application creates a reduced-resolution preview of that image for the page and a *link* back to the source of the original.

InDesign, QuarkXPress, and Illustrator identify linked files using their filenames and locations. Both InDesign and QuarkXPress have link management palettes that help you keep track of all pieces of artwork and their location.

When it's time to prepare your page layout for output, use the Package command (InDesign) or Prepare For Output (QuarkXPress) to assemble all the linked images and illustrations. These tools copy all the necessary files—including type fonts—into one folder so you can easily prepare a disc to send to your prepress provider.

InDesign also prepares an interactive *preflight report* that lists missing fonts or graphics, identifies incorrect color spaces (RGB in a CMYK document, for example), and allows you to repair your layout before committing to send your files to print.

Adobe Illustrator doesn't have a Package command; if you use Illustrator as your page-layout application, you must check all links and then carefully assemble all parts of your document to send for output.

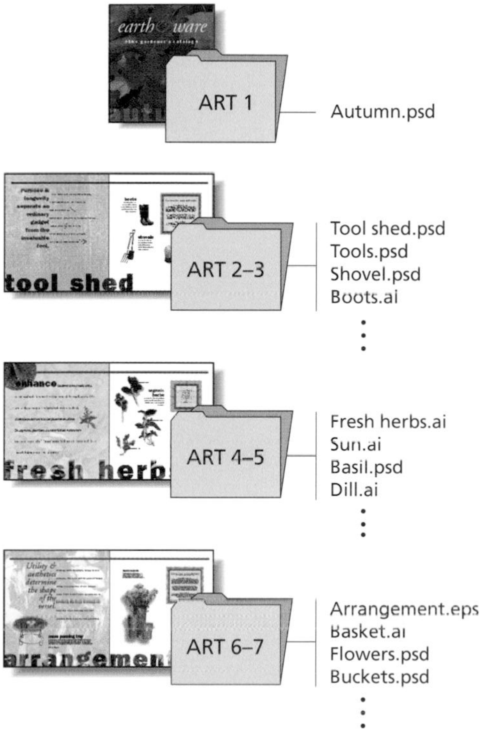

Organize your files as you construct your publication by setting up folders for art. Doing so will help you create a well-organized project. When you package your files for output, InDesign creates two folders: one for pictures and one for fonts. All contributing files are put into the correct folder.

Using Type

In the world of electronic publishing, type should look good onscreen and print flawlessly from output devices such as laser printers and platesetters. Unlike type that is cast in metal or imaged photographically, digital type gives you the means to control every aspect of typesetting.

Setting good-looking type

A sculpture's success depends not only on its shape and material but also on the space around it. Typography is no different—to communicate ideas, type must be readable as well as legible. *Legibility* refers to the ability to distinguish between letters; *readability* refers to ease of comprehension and reader comfort. Making type more readable involves the manipulation of type sizes and the space around letters, words, and lines of text.

The shapes of individual letters influence *kerning*. For instance, two letters with either curved or diagonal strokes that are set together require the least amount of space between them; combinations of straight vertical lines need the most space; and a curved or diagonal stroke next to a straight line needs a medium amount of space. The latest Adobe applications have both table-based kerning adjustments and optical kerning methods.

Adding or removing an equal amount of space between characters, usually in paragraphs of text, to achieve overall tighter or looser letterspacing is known as *tracking*. Type smaller than 10 points may require added space (positive tracking), whereas larger type sizes—over 18 points—may need less (negative tracking). Most page-layout programs include tracking capabilities; the way you perform this function varies by application, so refer to your user guide for details.

Reverse type—white type on a black background—might also require more space between letters. In this case, use positive tracking to improve legibility.

Your printing environment may also require adjustment of the overall tracking. If you're printing on absorbent paper, for instance, you may need to increase tracking to allow for ink spread that occurs during printing.

bo ok lin

The amount of space between letters depends on the shapes of the letter strokes. Use automatic kerning functions in your page-layout application to overcome unsightly kerning pairs in text.

A solar eclipse is a fairly rare occurrence. When they happen, the scientific community rushes to measure, while the curi-ous find clever filtration devices with which to observe the phenomenon. One must assume that in ancient times, people were similarly fascinated by the occasional event.

Warnock Pro 14 pt. (OpenType)
Tracked –12 units

A solar eclipse is a fairly rare occurrence. When they happen, the scien-tific community rushes to measure, while the curious find clever filtra-tion devices with which to observe the phenom-enon. One must assume that in ancient times, people were similarly fascinated by the occa-

Warnock Pro 14 pt. (OpenType)
Tracked +12 units

dahlia

–20 Tracking
Warnock Pro Light Italic Display (OpenType)

dahlia

–40 Tracking
Warnock Pro Light Italic Display (OpenType)

Word spacing

Words need to be far enough apart to be distinguished from one another but not so far that they separate into individual, unrelated units. That is, the spaces between words must be large enough to see individual word shapes, but the reader must also be able to group three or four words at a time for quick comprehension. The proper word spacing for unjustified text (in which the right margin is uneven or ragged) depends primarily on type size and line length.

If headlines are set in a large-size type—24 points, for example—little space is required between words; the space used by a 24-point lowercase *i* is a good gauge. In typical 12-point body text of ten words per line, however, more space between words is required. Most page-layout programs use the default word spacing provided in each typeface (which usually works well without adjustment in typical text settings); some allow you to adjust this spacing. Very short lines of text require tighter word spacing than the default.

Ta rv We gy RA 7, y.

Unkerned character pairs

Ta rv We gy RA 7, y.

Kerned character pairs

igjen igjen

Before kerning After kerning

CLIMATE CLIMATE

Before manual kerning: uneven fit

After manual kerning and tracking: more balanced spacing

AiJayiventuredaintoiaiyard

Headline word spacing

How PostScript printers use fonts

When you send a document to a PostScript printer, the printer uses the fonts it finds according to the following priorities:

1. Fonts that have been manually downloaded to the printer.
2. Fonts stored in the printer's read-only memory (ROM).
3. Fonts stored on a hard disk in or attached to the printer.
4. Fonts stored in the Mac OS or Windows system (these are downloaded by the printer driver when the job is sent to the printer).

If the printer can't find the font in any of these other locations, it usually substitutes the font Courier.

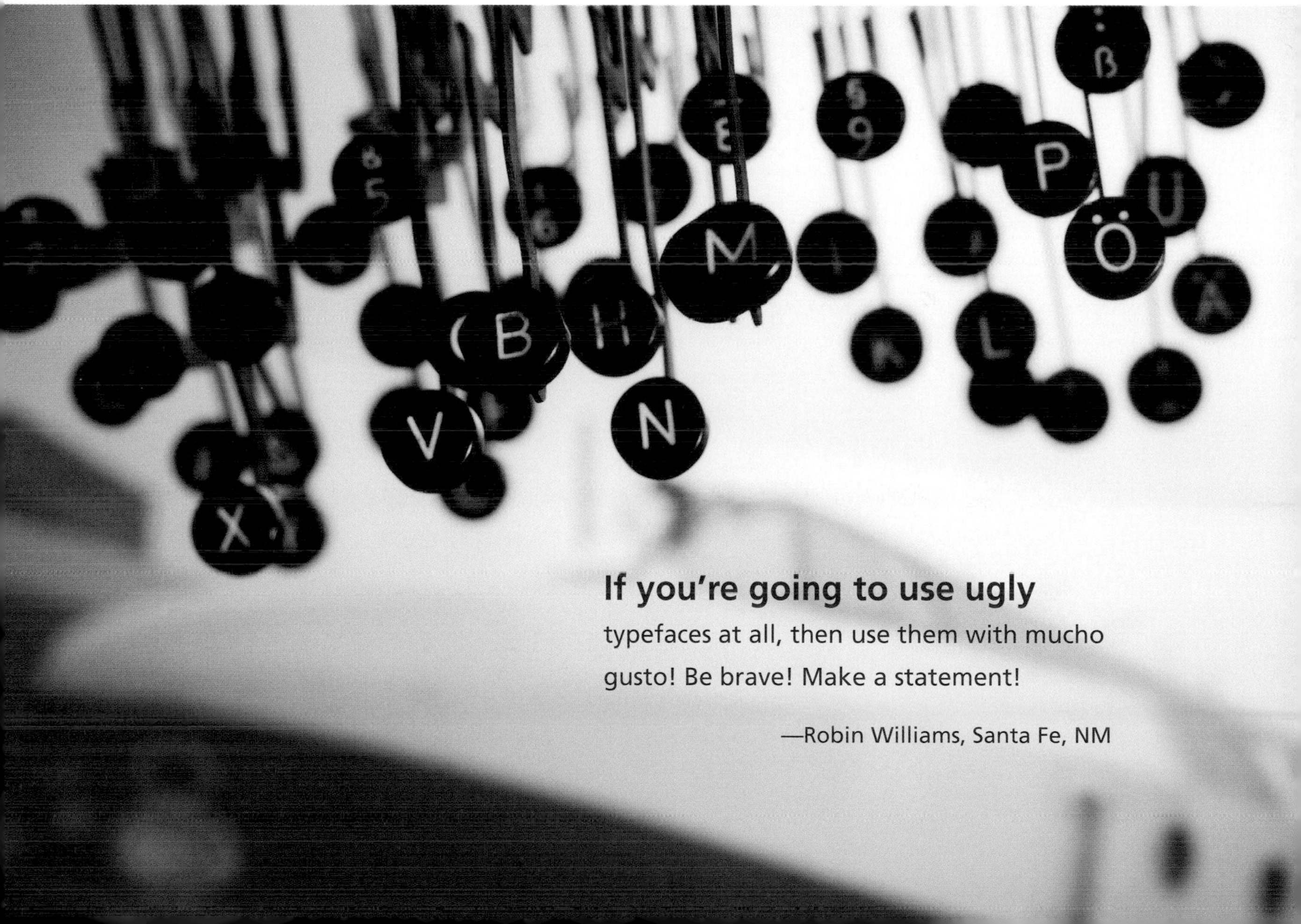

If you're going to use ugly typefaces at all, then use them with mucho gusto! Be brave! Make a statement!

—Robin Williams, Santa Fe, NM

Font Formats

As discussed earlier, OpenType fonts are the new industry standard for imaging to any PostScript output device. OpenType fonts are PostScript language-based outlines—object-oriented vector graphics—that can be scaled to any size and still remain sharp and smooth on any platform or output device.

Earlier font formats included Adobe Type 1 fonts, which are made up of two software components: the *screen font* and the *outline font* (these occasionally are called by different names: *bitmap font* and *printer font*). Type 1 fonts are limited to about 250 characters per font, but otherwise they deliver superb quality at any size. They are platform specific.

TrueType fonts are found on all Macintosh and Windows computers. They are usually shipped with the operating system, and they also produce excellent output on PostScript printers and platesetters. Like Type 1 fonts, the TrueType font has a character set of about 250 characters.

You can use OpenType, PostScript Type 1, and TrueType fonts interchangeably in page layouts. The advantages of OpenType are its large library of glyphs and alternate characters. In every other respect, the three font types should produce equal results and should print properly on all modern PostScript RIPs.

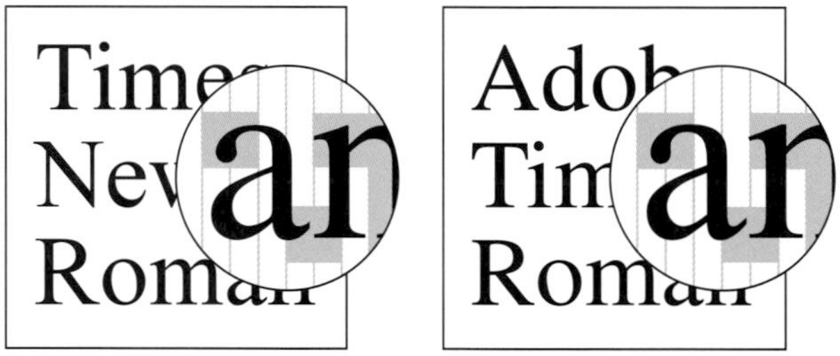

Fonts from different foundries may not have the same width and letterspacing characteristics—even if they share the same font name.

Medium

36pt Helvetica

Medium

24pt Helvetica

Medium

Create close relationships with knowledgeable and experienced production people, print brokers, and service bureaus. You can benefit from the combined expertise.

—Lori Barra, Sausalito, CA

Typographic Terms

When older typesetting methods gave way to electronic publishing, certain traditional terms got carried along. Today we use a mix of old and new terminology to describe typography.

Alignment The positioning of text within margins. Text flush with the margins on both sides is referred to as *justified.* Text is often aligned with only one margin, either the left or right and is then described as right- or left-justified, ragged left or -right, or flush-left or -right.

Ascender The stem of lowercase letters (such as k, b, and d) that ascends above the x-height of the other lowercase letters in a typeface.

Backslant A typeface with a backwards slant, the opposite of italic.

Baseline The imaginary line on which the majority of the characters in a typeface rest.

Body copy The main text of a document, as distinct from titles and headings.

Boldface A typeface rendered in darker, thicker strokes so that it will stand out.

Bullet A dot or other special character used to indicate items in a list.

Cap height The height from the baseline to the top of the uppercase letters in a font. This may or may not be the same as the height of ascenders.

Centered text Text placed at an equal distance from the left and right margins. Headlines are often centered.

Character In typography, a single element such as a letter, numeral, or mark of punctuation. The emerging term to describe these typographic elements is *glyph,* which is more descriptive when discussing non-Roman alphabet characters.

Character encoding An encoding is a table that maps character codes to the glyphs of a font. There are 32,768 possible typographic codes in the latest font technology, OpenType, designed to accommodate nearly any alphabet system known.

Condensed font A narrower version of a font that is used to get more characters into a given space.

Copyfitting A typographic process of adjusting the size and spacing of type to make it fit within a defined area or on a definite number of printed pages. Can be done by calculation, or by successive adjustments at the computer until a fit is reached.

Descender The part of a lowercase letter (such as y, p, and q) that descends below the baseline. In many typefaces, the uppercase J and Q also descend below the baseline.

Dingbats Non-alphanumeric glyphs. Dingbat fonts consisting entirely of these characters are a source of graphic symbols—such as arrows, bullets, and dividers—and other graphic ornaments.

Display type Type larger than that of the body text, used for headlines and display.

Drop cap A document style in which the first capital letter of a paragraph is set in a larger point size and aligned with the top of the first line. Used to indicate the start of a new section of text, such as a chapter.

Ellipsis A punctuation character consisting of three dots, or periods, in a row. It indicates that a word or phrase has been omitted.

Em, em space, em quad A common unit of measurement in typography. The em is the width of the point size. For example, in 12-point type, one em has a width of 12 points.

Em dash A dash the length of an em used to indicate a break in a sentence.

En, en space, en quad A common unit of measurement in typography. The en is typically half the width of the point size. It is half the width of an em space.

En dash A dash the length of an en is used to indicate a range of values. Some typographers prefer it to the longer em-dash to indicate a break in a sentence.

Flush-left ragged-right Text that is aligned on the left margin is said to be flush-left. If the text is unaligned on the right, so that it has a ragged edge, it is said to be flush-left ragged right. The term ragged-right is sometimes used alone to mean the same thing.

Flush-right ragged-left Text that is aligned on the right margin is said to be flush right and, if unaligned on the left, is said to be set flush-right ragged-left. The term ragged-left is sometimes used alone to mean the same thing.

Font One style, weight, and width of a typeface. An example is Times Bold Extended. Times is a typeface family, Roman is a style, Bold is a weight, Extended is a width. The terms font and typeface tend to be used interchangeably.

In hand-set type, the term *font* described *a single point size* of a particular typeface design. Because digital-typesetting technology enables scalable fonts, the size defining a font is no longer applicable.

Font contrast Font contrast refers to the range of thickness of the strokes used to draw a font's characters. Helvetica has low contrast, for example, because the letters are drawn with strokes of uniform thickness. Bodoni, on the other hand, has high contrast.

Font family Also called a *typeface family*. A collection of similar fonts designed to be used together. The Garamond family, for example, includes roman and italic styles, several weights (regular, semibold, and bold), and several widths (extended and compressed).

Galley proof A proof that is close enough to final copy to permit proofreading. The traditional galley was a small unit of machine-set type, which was checked before being merged into a frame with other galleys. The galley proof—also called a *reader's proof*—was used to check for errors in typesetting.

Typographic Terms (continued)

Glyph The basic building block in typesetting is a *glyph*—a letter, numeral, or symbol; groups of glyphs together are called *fonts.* One or more fonts sharing particular design features make up a family; Adobe *Myriad Pro,* for example, is the name of a type *family. Myriad Pro Regular* is an individual font within that family. The *Pro* in the name indicates that the font is an OpenType font.

New *Glyphs* palettes in InDesign, Illustrator and QuarkXPress allow for the selection of alternate characters from a palette showing all available alternate characters. Adobe now ships all of its fonts in OpenType format, and other type foundries are offering their fonts in this format in addition to the older Type 1 and TrueType font formats.

Greeking Gibberish used to take the place of real text for layout purposes.

Hanging indent A document style in which the first line of a paragraph is aligned with the left margin, and the remaining lines are all indented an equal amount. An effective style for displaying lists of information, sometimes referred to as *outdenting.*

Italic A slanting or script-like version of a face. The upright faces are often referred to as Roman.

Justified In typography, text is justified if it is flush on both the left and right margins. Text that is *flush-right* or *flush-left,* in other words aligned on only one margin, is sometimes described as being *right-justified* or *left-justified.*

Kerning The adjustment of horizontal space between pairs of characters to create a perception of uniformity; critical where large typefaces are used, as in headlines. The letters Ty would require kerning to tuck the y under the wing of the T.

Keyboard layout, keyboard mapping
A keyboard layout or mapping is the table governing which character is generated when a particular key or combination of keys is pressed.

Letterspacing Letterspacing adjustments are applied to a block of text as a whole, and are sometimes referred to as *tracking.* This is distinct from kerning, which adjusts space between pairs of letters. Letterspacing is used to improve legibility and to fit more or less text into the given space.

Ligature Two or more letters drawn as a unit. In some typefaces, certain pairs of letters overlap in unsightly ways if printed side by side. Substituting a ligature improves the appearance in these cases. Examples include the *fi*,and *fl* pairs.

Oblique A slanting version of a face. Oblique is similar to italic but without the script quality of a true italic.

OpenType OpenType solves the problems of previous font technologies. OpenType fonts are cross-platform and can contain character sets of tens of thousands of glyphs, allowing for typography in almost any language. Special characters, such as small caps and old-style numerals are included in OpenType fonts rather than being found in a separate font. In addition to scalable OpenType fonts, Adobe offers *Opticals,* series of OpenType fonts that are designed for setting in a narrow range of point sizes.

MyriadPro-Cond.otf

Paragraph rules Graphic lines that separate blocks of text and isolate graphics on a page.

Pi characters Special typographic characters, such as mathematical symbols, not included in ordinary fonts.

Pica A unit of measure that is approximately one-sixth of an inch. A pica is equal to 12 points. The traditional British and American pica is 0.166 inch. In PostScript devices, a pica is exactly 1/6 inch.

Point A unit of measure in typography. The original ANSI point was 72.27 to the inch, but the PostScript era ushered-in a new point that is exactly 72 to the inch.

Point size The common way to describe the size of a font. A font's point size is the distance in points from the top of the highest ascender to the bottom of the lowest descender plus a tiny gap for legibility.

Quad A typesetting term for a specified space size. For example, an em quad is the width of the point size, and an en quad is half that width.

Raised cap A design style in which the first capital letter of a paragraph is set in a large point size and aligned with the baseline of the first line of text. Compare to a drop cap.

Reverse type, reverse text Type that is printed white on black, or light-colored against a dark background.

Roman The upright style of a typeface, as contrasted with its italic version.

Sans-serif font A typeface without serifs, the tiny ornaments that are found on the tips of letter parts. Helvetica is an example of a sans-serif font.

Serif In typeface design, a small, decorative stroke appearing at the ends of the main strokes that define a letter.

Typographic Terms (continued)

Strike-through Text that has a line drawn through every letter, essentially showing cancellation. The technique is used when editing a document, and in legal printing, where the original text is shown, with strike-through, and the replacement text is printed nearby.

Style One of the variations, such as italic and bold, that comprise a typeface family.

Symbol font A font consisting primarily of mathematical symbols rather than ordinary letters and numbers. See *pi characters.*

Tabular figures Numerals that all have the same width. This makes it easier to set tables of data. Also called *lining numerals.*

Tracking The average space between characters in a block of text. Sometimes also referred to as letterspacing.

TrueType A scalable type technology.

Type 1 A standard format for digital type. Originally developed by Adobe, Type 1 was, until recently, the most commonly available digital type format. Type 1 has been replaced by OpenType fonts, which offer many more characters, multiple-language support, and stretchable elements for setting music and text in languages with such elements.

Typeface A design for the letters, numbers, and symbols comprising a font, often part of a family of coordinated designs. Individual typefaces are usually identified by a family name and some additional terms indicating style, weight, and width.

Typeface family *See* font family.

Typeface styles Within a typeface family, variants such as Roman and Italic.

Typeface weights Variants within a single typeface family, including thin, light, bold, extra-bold, and black.

Typeface widths Width variants within a single typeface family, including extended, condensed, and normal width.

Typographic "color" The consistency of a block of text. This depends on the thickness of the strokes that make up the characters, as well as the point size and leading used for setting the text block. When seasoned typographers refer to "color," they are talking about textual consistency, the lack of rivers of white space in composed text, and evenness.

Widow A single word or part of a word ending a paragraph of type.

Word-spacing Adjusting the average distance between words to improve legibility or to fit a block of text into a given amount of space.

X-height Traditionally, x-height is the height of the lowercase letter *x*. As a general rule, it is the height of the body of lowercase letters in a font, excluding the ascenders and descenders. Some lowercase letters may extend a little bit above or below the x-height as part of their design, even without ascenders and descenders. The x-height can vary considerably among typefaces with the same point size, which is based on the width of certain uppercase letters.

Tips for Working with Page-Layout Files

Generally speaking, these suggestions apply to creating documents in any page-layout program. Some may also be applicable if you're designing individual pages in an illustrator program.

Create a project folder. Before you begin a project, create a folder in which to store your publication and its linked files, such as images and fonts. Meticulous organization of files can prevent trouble at the last minute.

Maintain a backup copy. System errors can happen unexpectedly. To prevent losing your work if an error occurs while you're in a publication, always create a backup copy of the publication and update it frequently.

Save your publication frequently. Save your publication immediately after you create it. Then, save it again each time you make changes that would be difficult or time-consuming to re-create. In the event of a power failure or system error, saving your publication frequently ensures you won't lose many changes.

Choose the correct graphic format. Most software applications support a variety of graphic file formats. Make sure the format you're using is compatible with the system doing the final imaging. Recent changes in the world of graphic arts preparation on computers favor files in their native format over generic files. Adobe InDesign and the recent release of QuarkXPress both support native Adobe Photoshop files; InDesign works better with native Illustrator files than it does with the more conventional .eps variety.

If you're working with digital images from cameras or scanners, you should work with either Photoshop native files (.psd) or TIFF files, because these are the most flexible formats.

Always place graphics and text rather than pasting them. Using graphics that are linked to the layout rather than pasted in ensures that the graphics will be printed at full resolution and that all editing capabilities will be available. For example, an image placed into an InDesign layout can be edited directly from InDesign; the edited image is updated automatically. Placed text is filtered by the page-layout application, and typographic details—like correct quotation marks and apostrophes—are substituted automatically as the text is brought into the page.

Run a preflight test prior to printing. To ensure that your publication prints correctly, verify that all your links are intact by running a preflight test. Adobe InDesign and QuarkXPress both offer windows that indicate whether a linked file is current, available, and ready for output.

Case Study: Dora Drimalas

Nike, the world's largest manufacturer of athletic sportswear, wants to make a splash when it talks to the press. So the company worked with Hybrid Design, a San Francisco-based design firm, to prepare a series of press kits that would get the attention of the media.

Dora Drimalas, Partner and Creative Director at Hybrid Design, chose to produce a series of poured clear acrylic cases into which were inserted three different press kits. The firm hired New York photographer Carlos Serrao to photograph cyclist Lance Armstrong, tennis champion Serena Williams, and runner Marion Jones wearing Nike sportswear for the campaign that led up to the Olympic games.

Drimalas explains that the idea for the plastic cases came from the style of Serrao's action photos. "We took a shard from the image and created the 'moment frozen in time' press kit. Part of the message focused on the fact that in Olympic competition, every hundredth of a second counts," says Drimalas. In each of the kits, the firm contrasted the exciting exterior photos with humanizing facts and figures about athletes and competition.

The outer sheet of each kit was screen-printed on acetate, while the interior cards were printed by offset lithography in process color, plus one spot color and a gloss varnish. The spot color was a custom mix with a pearlescent finish. Included in the kit was a CD meticulously screen-printed with colors to match the offset cards.

For another press kit series, the firm chose a blind-embossed box to make a statement about speed. The box was printed with two passes of red ink and a UV coating on the exterior, plus two coats of silver and a satin-finish UV coating on the interior before being embossed. Then the word "speed" in many languages was embossed deeply into the paper. Drimalas describes the process: "The emboss was hit as hard as we could without ripping through the paper. This is when it starts to feel like a sculpture. That's where it makes the best impression."

Surely, handling the design for a firm like Nike requires attention to detail. Says Drimalas of the process, "We make meticulously clean files, properly labeled discs, correct links, correctly labeled Pantone colors, properly gathered fonts. We work with the best printers in the world, and we have to give them world-class work to print. Nothing is left to chance."

She explains that part of the company's success comes from pushing the limits of production by "finding a printer who is open to new technologies and trying new techniques on-press. And we have open and continuous dialog from start to finish."

When asked if she has advice for others preparing artwork for printing, Drimalas says that continuous proofing is one key to success. "We have many people proof our projects before they go out. An extra set of eyes is always helpful."

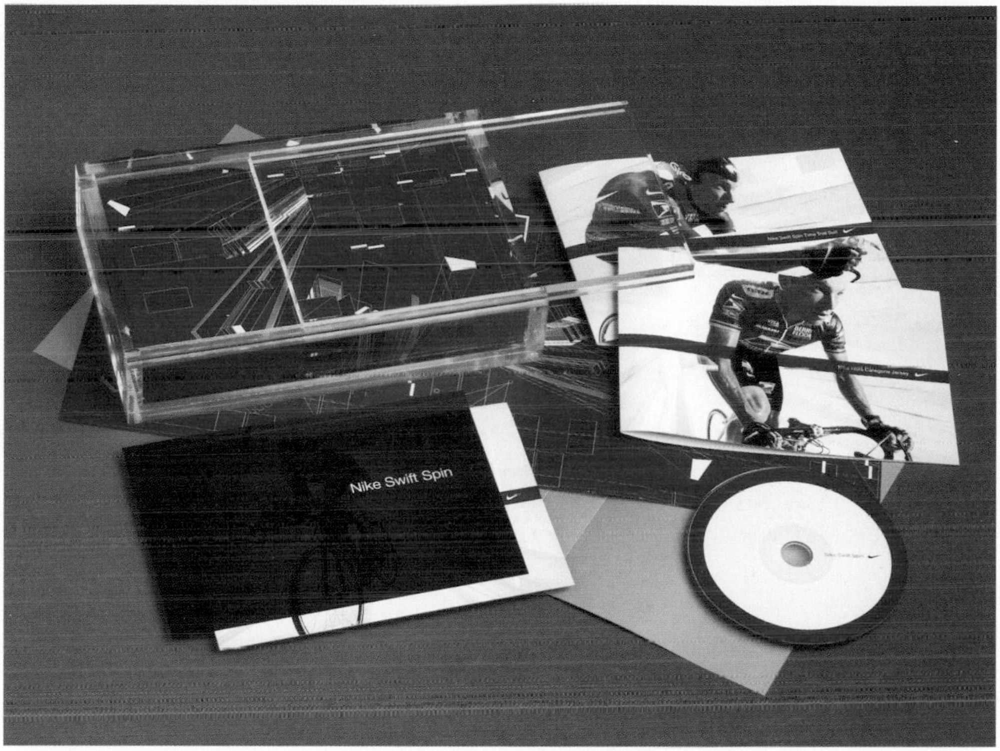

All of the production on these projects for was done with Adobe Illustrator and Adobe Photoshop. Printing was done by Cenveo, South San Francisco, California.

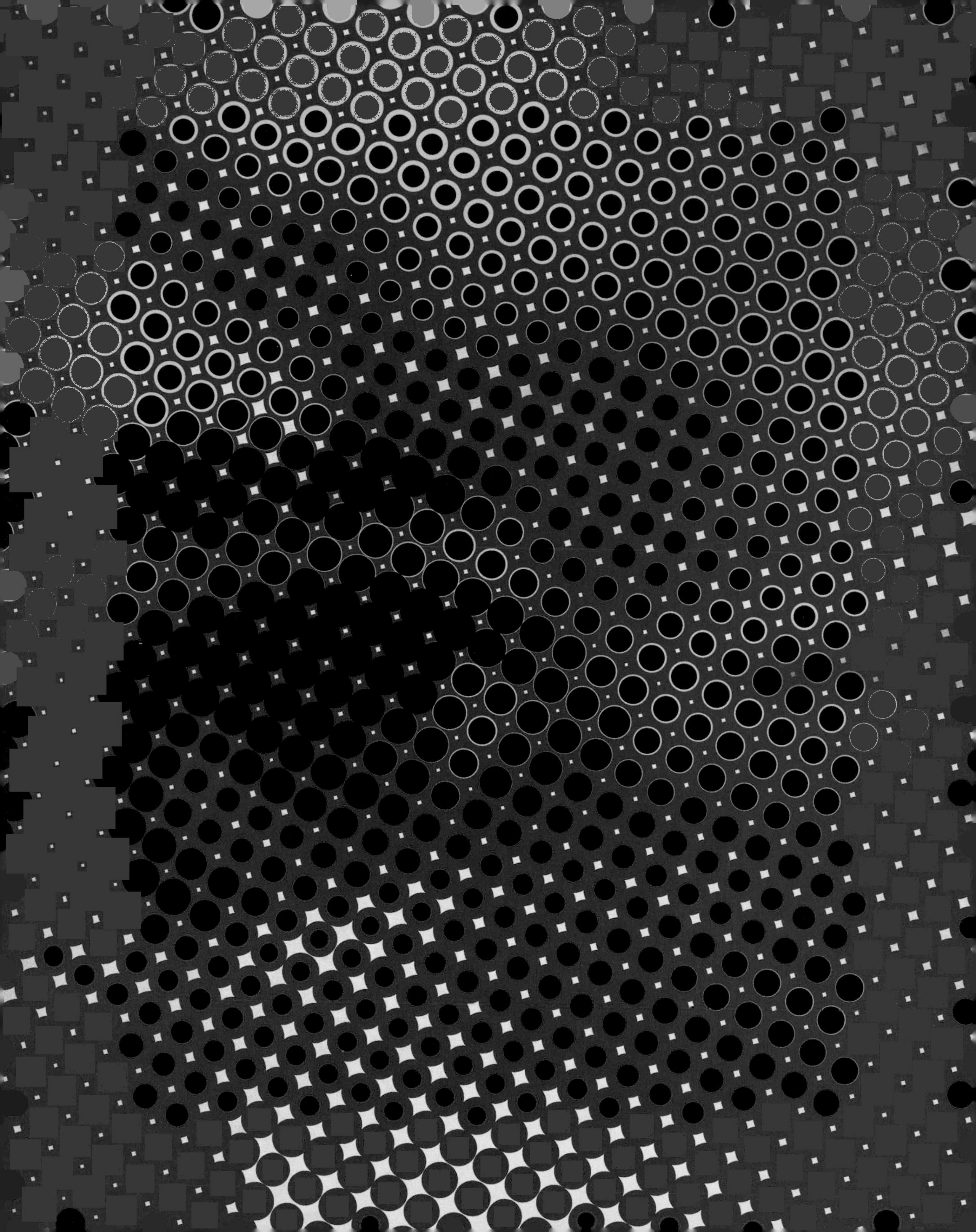

3 Imaging and Proofing

Desktop Proofing Options

What to Send to Production

Checking Your Files

Including a Report

Color Proofing

Types of Proofs

Checking Color Proofs

Color Bars

Archiving Your Work

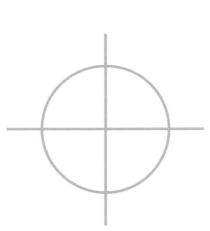

Imaging and Proofing

Checking your finished files, proofing them locally, and handing them off for production are three key steps in the final production cycle.

A final check prior to handoff ordinarily includes printing a proof copy on your desktop printer. Although inspecting a desktop copy isn't the same as getting actual proofs from the printer, you can think of it as the first of several stages of proofing. Prior to handoff, it's equally important to verify that your files are complete before putting them into production.

Turning over your files for imaging involves collecting images, illustrations, fonts, and layout documents and organizing them for production. Adobe InDesign and QuarkXPress both offer software tools for collecting the components of a project, assembling them into folders of associated documents, and making them ready for print production.

Many printing firms also accept print-ready Adobe PDF files created from the page-layout application. PDF documents can be made with full-resolution images and embedded fonts, and they can optionally be converted to the correct color type for printing on a specific press and paper combination using an ICC profile recommended by your printer.

Desktop Proofing Options

Preview your publication throughout its development as a way to check the layout, verify the accuracy of text and graphics, and solve potential printing problems before the files are imaged. You can use a color desktop printer to print a composite proof, giving you an idea what the completed project will look like. You can also use a desktop printer to print color separations to see whether objects print on the correct separations.

Problems identified in a desktop proof can be corrected quickly and easily; the same problems identified on press are dramatically more expensive to fix. Many prepress service providers require a desktop printer proof when you deliver your files for production.

You should make numerous proofs as you develop your publication. Get technical input from your customer as you go to eliminate errors. The services of a professional editor and proofreader are worth the cost.

Virtual proof (onscreen or soft proof)

WHAT IT IS

An onscreen preview lets you examine the pages of your publication on your computer display.

APPROPRIATE USES

Use periodic onscreen proofs to refine the appearance of text and to check the overall layout. Enlarge critical areas to get a better look. Check to see that the correct colors have been assigned to each object.

Adobe Creative Suite applications offer a **Proof Colors** option, which activates a selected output color profile and then shows the document on the computer display with realistic color. Adobe InDesign can also simulate the color of the paper based on the **paper white** reading made when the profile was created. The default profile is defined in the Suite Color Settings found in Adobe Bridge software. Each application can override the default settings for customized color proofing.

You can also make a color-accurate virtual proof using a properly prepared Adobe PDF document viewed on a calibrated and profiled computer display. Special virtual-proofing software can create proofs of adequate quality to replace the prepress proofs traditionally made before printing.

Desktop laser proof

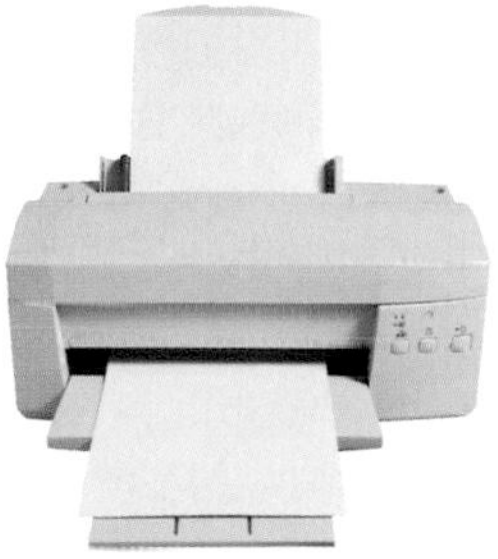

WHAT IT IS

Black-and-white composite prints are printed on a PostScript laser printer. This is an inexpensive way to identify problems with layout and design. By printing color separations, you can verify that objects have been assigned the correct colors in your document.

APPROPRIATE USES

Check registration marks and crop marks. You may need to reduce the size of the printed piece to fit on desktop printer paper, but even a reduced-size proof is a valuable aid in finding and correcting errors prior to a press run.

Desktop color proof

WHAT IT IS

A composite proof printed on a PostScript color printer can be a good preliminary proof. High-resolution (1440–2880 dpi) inkjet printers can also generate good preliminary proofs.

APPROPRIATE USES

Composite proofs from a desktop color printer are useful for previewing page design, showing color relationships, and verifying image quality. These composites have the disadvantage of not letting you anticipate some press problems, such as moiré patterns and register error. And most color composite proofs can't show color trapping. In addition, unless you've been using a color-managed workflow, the colors in your composite proofs may be unreliable.

What to Send to Production

Your files are in the format specific to that particular application. At handoff, you may choose to transfer your files as they are—in Adobe InDesign or QuarkXPress—or you may choose to convert them to Adobe PDF format. Both approaches offer advantages.

Transferring files in their native form

Handing off a file in the format of your page-layout program allows the service bureau to run its own preflight check on your file, making sure that linked files are present and that all fonts are available. Your service provider will also select the correct printing options for the job: printer's marks, screen ruling, bleed, and any additional controls needed to print to their platesetter. If service providers encounter problems, they can usually troubleshoot the files and fix them (there is a charge for this service).

Before you hand off any document for production, be sure to communicate with the production specialists about the software you're using and your computer platform. Although there are few problems relating to applications or computer platforms today, it's nice to check in advance.

Converting to Adobe PDF

If your service provider uses a PDF workflow for print production, you can provide complete Adobe PDF files, ready to print. Many graphic arts firms use PDF-based workflows for graphic arts–quality productions.

If you use Adobe InDesign, you can choose one of several *PDF presets* to make your PDF files directly from that application. QuarkXPress also has a method for making PDF files directly from the application. To ensure maximum compatibility, set the preference in QuarkXPress to use an external PDF application—specifically, *Distiller*, which is part of the Adobe Acrobat software package.

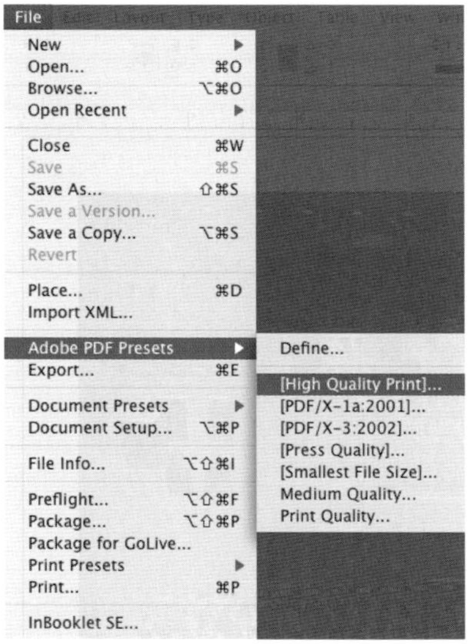

Two graphic arts–specific PDF types are used in the graphic arts industry:

- *PDF/X-1a* is a PDF specification that ensures compatibility with SWOP-standard printing production systems. It forces a document to CMYK color and forces compliance with resolution standards that are minimal for SWOP printing. PDF/X-1a is a good choice if your work is destined to be run as an advertisement in a publication, or if your work is to be run on a web-fed offset press, on a rotogravure press, or sheet-fed with SWOP standards.
- *PDF/X-3* is a more advanced PDF standard. It's designed for graphic arts–quality production, but it acknowledges more than four colors—thus enabling spot colors, varnishes, and so on. PDF/X3 also allows RGB files to be part of a graphic arts document, with ICC profiles embedded for later processing to CMYK for print by the printing company.

Choosing either one is appropriate for print, but it's important to ask your commercial printer which type of PDF they prefer before committing to making the documents. You may also find that your commercial printer has its own recommendations for making PDF files ready for printing.

Also remember that PDF creation for print usually leaves photos in the document uncompressed, which can cause these files to be very large. Don't expect the compact files you get when you compress to PDF for Internet or business document delivery. A 50 MB PDF file for a single-page color document isn't unreasonable.

Checking Your Files

When it's time to hand off your document to your prepress service provider, a systematic check of your files helps to ensure that your document will print from another computer. This process, analogous to a pilot's preflight check, is intended to catch missing files, missing fonts, material not intended for print, and any components that may prevent the document from imaging correctly.

Adobe InDesign has a *Preflight* function that evaluates all the components of your document and produces a report showing real and potential problems. This preflight report is interactive: double-clicking any reported problem leads you to the offending item, allowing for changes if necessary. Some reported problems—like RGB color images in a color-managed workflow—may not be problems at all, so you can skip them if you're confident that they don't represent an obstacle to production.

After you've checked your files, make a final proof of them on a PostScript laser printer, if available. Printing on a PostScript printer will help to identify any problems that might occur on a PostScript platesetter at the printing firm.

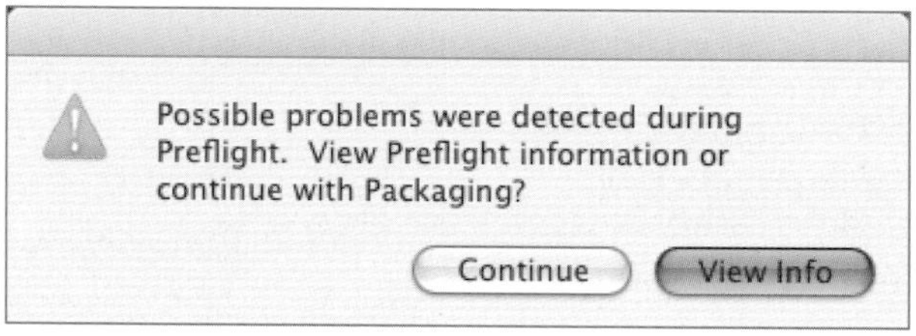

Checking files before going to press

- Check to be sure you have the correct number of pages. Delete any blank or unnecessary pages. If you're printing an imposed multipage publication, be aware that the total count of pages must be divisible by four (sometimes eight) to fold into efficient signatures.
- Remove artwork that may have been placed in the layout but isn't used in the final document. Remember that some artwork items marked "do not print" may have important placeholder purposes; these should remain in the document.
- Check linked graphics to ensure that you're using the latest versions.
- Verify that all colors are defined and named correctly. If you're using spot colors, make sure that each is defined with just one name.
- Check bleeds and traps. Make sure that bleed allowances are sufficient (usually .125 inch) and that trapping specifications are correct.

Organizing and packaging files

- Using the *Package* function in InDesign or the *Collect for Output* function in QuarkXPress, copy all art files and fonts into a new folder on your hard drive. Then, close the document and reopen it from the copy in the folder you just created. Doing so tests the links in your document. After this process is complete, copy the folder to a CD-ROM or DVD-ROM; both are excellent for the transfer of publications.
- If possible, open the document on another computer in your workplace, using the CD-ROM you created. Doing so helps to uncover any font problems and indicates problems with missing or modified images and graphics.
- Many printing companies provide online file-delivery systems or FTP sites for the transfer of your documents. Use an FTP client or a Web browser to make the transfer. If file security is a concern, you should hand-deliver the disc to the printing firm or ask the company to provide access to a secure FTP server that can't be accessed by others.

Including a Report

Plan to give a printed copy of your document and a printed report of all its requirements and settings to your prepress service provider. The report gives your service provider and commercial printer an understanding of your project. InDesign has an online *Instructions* form that you fill in as you're packaging your document for production. This document travels with the job and can be opened and used by the prepress specialists to enter basic information about your job into their production system. The Instructions form is one entry point to a state-of-the-art system called Job Description Format (JDF), where prepress equipment, presses, bindery equipment, and accounting systems all exchange information about your job; this system allows for better production efficiencies and cost accounting.

Packaging your job for production also generates a report in the same folder as the document, outlining the contents of the document—from page size and number of colors, to a complete list of linked graphics and fonts. This report is an orderly listing of the details of your document. Include a printed copy of your document and a pagination sheet. If your document folds, be sure to include a folded laser output mock-up of the project.

In addition to your service report, you should include a specification sheet for your commercial printer. The specification sheet should include this publication specifications information:

Settings for imaging. On the mock-up of your document, be sure to indicate the paper weight, the surface and paper brand you've agreed to with your prepress service provider, the halftone screen frequency, any ICC profiles used, and whether you've done any trapping in the document.

Font list. List all fonts used in the document and any fonts included in imported artwork. This information is included automatically in the report generated by the page-layout application.

Detailed page listing. Print out all pages of your publication, including both blank and numbered pages. Use the page numbers to keep track of special requirements on each page. Indicate sections, chapters, or other breaks in long publications.

Number of colors. If you're printing color, indicate the number of colors that need to be printed for each page. This number should also include any spot colors or varnishes on the page.

Notes. Include notes to remind yourself of any special handling on a page. Note the location of bleeds, crossovers, and areas in the publication that need special attention.

Also include the following information on your specification sheet:

- Printing specifications (trim size, quantity, binding process, and so on)
- Packing and shipping instructions
- Due date
- Contact information (how to get in touch with you)

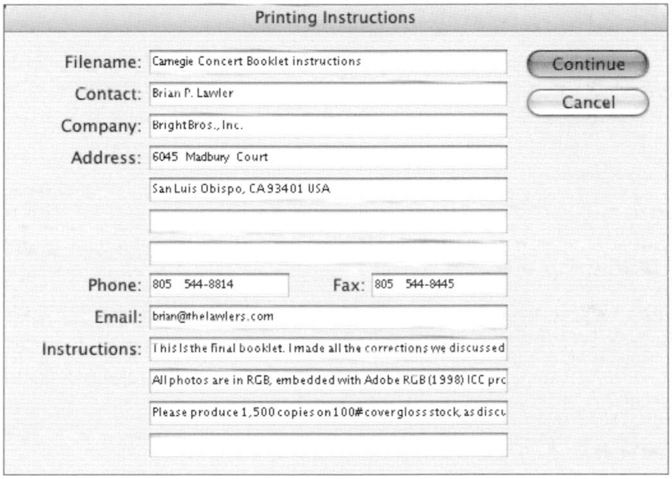

Sample service provider report

Following is the text of an InDesign document, ready for print. It includes most of the specifications for production and printing, a complete listing of linked graphics, fonts, colors used, and contact information:

ADOBE INDESIGN PRINTING INSTRUCTIONS FOR
SERVICE PROVIDER REPORT
PUBLICATION NAME: Photo Flyer.indd

PACKAGE DATE: 5/24/05 12:36 AM

Creation Date: 5/19/05

Modification Date: 5/20/05

CONTACT INFORMATION

Company Name: Bright Bros., Inc.
Contact: Brian P. Lawler
Address:
6045 Madbury Court
San Luis Obispo, CA 93401 USA

Phone: 805 544-8814
Fax: 805 544-8445
Email: brian@thelawlers.com

SPECIAL INSTRUCTIONS AND OTHER NOTES

This is the final booklet. I made all the changes we discussed, and here it is!

All photos are in RGB, embedded with Adobe RGB (1998) ICC profiles. Please use your gloss paper profile when printing, as we discussed.

Please produce 2,500 copies on 100# cover gloss stock, as discussed.

External Plug-ins 1
InBooklet SE.4x.pln.framework

Non Opaque Objects :None
FONTS
3 Fonts Used; 0 Missing, 1 Embedded, 0 Incomplete, 0 Protected

Fonts Packaged
- Name: MinionPro-Bold; Type: OpenType Type 1, Status: OK
- Name: MinionPro-Regular; Type: OpenType Type 1, Status: OK
- Name: MyriadPro-Black; Type: Type 1, Status: Embedded

COLORS AND INKS
4 Process Inks; 0 Spot Inks

- Name and Type: Process Cyan; Angle: 45.000; Lines/Inch: 60.000
- Name and Type: Process Magenta; Angle: 45.000; Lines/Inch: 60.000
- Name and Type: Process Yellow; Angle: 45.000; Lines/Inch: 60.000
- Name and Type: Process Black; Angle: 45.000; Lines/Inch: 60.000

LINKS AND IMAGES
(Missing & Embedded Links Only)
Links and Images: 24 Links Found; 0 Modified, 0 Missing
Images: 0 Embedded, 23 use RGB color space

PRINT SETTINGS
PPD: Xerox Phaser 7700DN, (Phaser 7700DN)
Printing To: Printer
Number of Copies: 1
Reader Spreads: No
Even/Odd Pages: Both
Pages: All
Proof: No
Tiling: None
Scale: 100%, 100%
Page Position: Upper Left
Printer's Marks: None
Bleed: .125 in, .125 in, .125 in, .125 in
Color: Composite CMYK
Trapping Mode: None
Send Image Data: Full Resolution
OPI/DCS Image Replacement: No
Page Size: Tabloid
Paper Dimensions: 11 in x 17 in
Orientation: Landscape
Negative: No
Flip Mode: Off

FILE PACKAGE LIST
1. Photo Flyer.indd; type: Adobe InDesign publication; size: 22791K
2. MinionPro-Bold.otf; type: Font file; size: 203K
3. MinionPro-Regular.otf; type: Font file; size: 199K
4. Carnegie Hall head.ai; type: Linked file; size: 217K
5. Carnegie-Hall-Exterior-3-22-05-03.psd; type: Linked file; size: 3163K
6. Carnegie-Hall-Marquee-3-22-05-05.psd; type: Linked file; size: 46109K
7. Manhattan-cruise-3-24-05-01.psd; type: Linked file; size: 46880K
8. Manhattan-skyline-3-24-05-06.psd; type: Linked file; size: 38358K
9. SLOHS Choir Send-off 3-13-05 60.psd; type: Linked file; size: 3363K
10. SLOHS-MBHS.jpg; type: Linked file; size: 1141K
11. SLOMBY-Choir-NYC-3-19-05-05.psd; type: Linked file; size: 46713K
12. SLOMBY-Choir-NYC-3-20-05-57.psd; type: Linked file; size: 42373K
13. SLOMBY-Choir-NYC-3-20-05-73.psd; type: Linked file; size: 47506K
14. SLOMBY-Choir-NYC-3-20-05-96.psd; type: Linked file; size: 44460K
15. SLOMBY-Choir-NYC-3-21-05-105.psd; type: Linked file; size: 48428K
16. SLOMBY-Choir-NYC-3-21-05-12.psd; type: Linked file; size: 46308K
17. SLOMBY-Choir-NYC-3-21-05-42.psd; type: Linked file; size: 8258K
18. SLOMBY-Choir-NYC-3-21-05-43.psd; type: Linked file; size: 8193K
19. SLOMBY-Choir-NYC-3-21-05-44.psd; type: Linked file; size: 8225K
20. SLOMBY-Choir-NYC-3-21-05-45.psd; type: Linked file; size: 8255K
21. SLOMBY-Choir-NYC-3-21-05-46.psd; type: Linked file; size: 8116K
22. SLOMBY-Choir-NYC-3-21-05-47.psd; type: Linked file; size: 8175K
23. SLOMBY-Choir-NYC-3-21-05-48.psd; type: Linked file; size: 8197K
24. SLOMBY-Choir-NYC-3-21-05-49.psd; type: Linked file; size: 8195K
25. SLOMBY-Choir-NYC-3-21-05-50.psd; type: Linked file; size: 8179K
26. SLOMBY-Choir-NYC-3-21-05-51.psd; type: Linked file; size: 8186K
27. Statue-of-Liberty-3-24-05-06.psd; type: Linked file; size: 28964

Color Proofing

Next to proofs made from the printing plates themselves, the most accurate proofs are made on wide-format ink-jet printers. These proofs accurately represent the color that the press will deliver, although sometimes the paper substrate used for proofing is whiter than your chosen printing paper. Such proofs are often used as contract proofs to indicate to the printer the color that you expect to see in the final press run.

As a general rule, the closer the proofing method mimics the conditions of the printing press, the more reliably it indicates the final product's quality. Most color proofing systems are optimized for process color printing; some proofing systems can also proof high-fidelity colors and spot colors. For spot colors, you can also get a *drawdown*—a smear of ink produced on the paper to be used—to verify quality and tone. Consult your vendors to see what proofing options are available.

The final stage of proofing is not only for checking your work but also for checking the printer's work. Without a contract proof, it may be difficult to settle disputes with the printer about color quality. The proof serves as an agreement between the printer and the customer and as a guide for adjusting the press during a press run.

Some people prefer to make a *press check,* visiting the printer's facility as the job is ready to print to approve the job as it comes off the press. This step is less common in the era of virtual (onscreen) proofing and highly accurate ink-jet prepress proofs, but it's always an option. However, changes made during this press check can be *very expensive,* because they may require making new printing plates and result in press downtime.

Try to keep an "anything is possible" attitude regarding color. Push the limits. Then proof, proof, and proof again.

—Mark Landkamer, Landkamer Partners,
San Francisco, CA

Types of proofs

Photomechanical proofs

Photomechanical laminate proofs are created by exposing each color separation on a layer of pigmented material and then laminating the layers together. Examples are Fuji Color-Art, DuPont Waterproof and Cromalin, Matchprint, and Agfa.

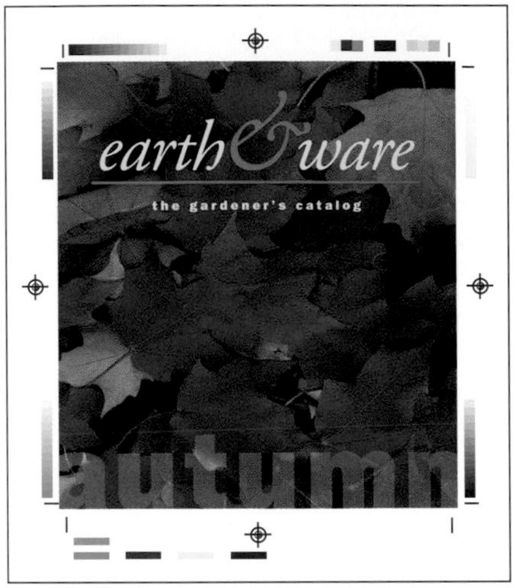

Laminate proofs are used for color forecasting and to identify moiré problems. Except in the case of a few printers that still use film imagesetters, laminate proofs generally aren't made today; they're costly and time-consuming to make.

Most printers—especially those using computer-to-plate systems—have switched to some form of digitally prepared proof. Many are moving to onscreen *virtual proofs*.

Digital ink-jet proofs

Digital proofs are usually created using pigments or dyes on wide-format ink-jet printers driven by a PostScript (Raster Image Processor (RIP).

Digital ink-jet proofing can achieve high quality and can sometimes use the actual paper stock you intend to print on rather than special sheets of material. However, most digital proofs don't show moirés and register error.

Some printers use high-resolution dye-sublimation printers to generate proofs. A number of these devices can mimic the halftone patterns of the platesetter.

Bluelines

Bluelines are diazo contact prints made from film separations produced on an imagesetter. They're seldom made today, because the industry is nearly 100 percent digital (and film is no longer made in most plants).

Bluelines are made on paper the same dimensions as the press sheet, which can be folded and bound so that you can check crossovers, bleeds, and page sequence. Bluelines are commonly produced for one-color or two-color publications as well as four-color process jobs. They're exposed and processed in the vacuum frame at the printing plant and require no processing; they also fade quickly.

Press proofs and press checks

For a press proof, plates are exposed, and the printer sets up the press to print a short run of the actual sheet. Changes to the job after press proofing require new plates to be made—a process that is usually prohibitively expensive.

A more common practice is a press check where the printer prepares the press using the final plates and an approved digital color proof. A designer or production person checks the early press sheets and signs off on an approved press sheet. The press sheet is then compared to sheets throughout the press run to ensure consistency.

Checking color proofs

With the availability of high quality low-cost desktop color printers, it's possible to make excellent proofs periodically during the design phase of a project. As you get close to completion, it's important to make proofs to check for color quality, content, and technical factors.

What to look for on a desktop color proof

- Check that colors are consistent throughout the pages.
- Check *memory* colors—that is, colors that are expected to look a certain way: skin tones, sky, grass, and so on. If these colors are off, the whole piece will be perceived to be incorrect.
- Check colors selected from color-matching systems against printed swatches.
- Make sure that bleeds and crossovers extend the required amount beyond the page margins.

What to look for on a prepress proof

When you're reviewing prepress proofs, which are made on one of a variety of wide-format ink-jet printers, or actual printed sheets at a press check, you must be on the lookout for certain problems. It will help to check your proofs in a viewing booth, with ISO-standard 5,000 Kelvin lighting.

- Digitally prepared prepress proofs usually have no halftone dots. Ink-jet proofs should be evaluated for color quality and overall appearance. The halftone patterns will show up later on the press.
- Look for missing copy elements, overprint characteristics, the quality of the black ink, and the black ink's relationship to other inks it overprints.
- Check to see that images are positioned correctly and that very small positional errors haven't crept into your production. Sometimes hair-thin lines appear along the edge of photo frames and aren't easily detected in the electronic—or even the onscreen—version of the document.
- Look for color casts in images or an overall cast to the document's illustrations and photos. This could be an indication that something is amiss with your computer display and its ability to show color correctly.

- Scan your copy for hyphenation errors, odd line endings, and dangling widows and orphans (words or parts of words left over after a page or column change). Proofreaders look for details like correct apostrophes and quotation marks. They also like prepositions to fall in-line with the phrases they introduce (don't leave *of* at the end of one line with its phrase continuing a line below). Double spaces anywhere in your document are inappropriate in excellent typography; this is a chance to catch these gaps and repair them. Making changes to copy is easy and relatively inexpensive at this stage.
- Check all addresses and phone numbers. Actually *call* the numbers to be sure they're working. Test all email addresses and Web addresses.
- Check all pages for correct bleeds, crossovers, and page numbers. Be sure page numbers print in the right place and that they're easily found when you're reading the printed product. Consider what happens if your page is folded or trimmed slightly wrong: will the page numbers be cut off?

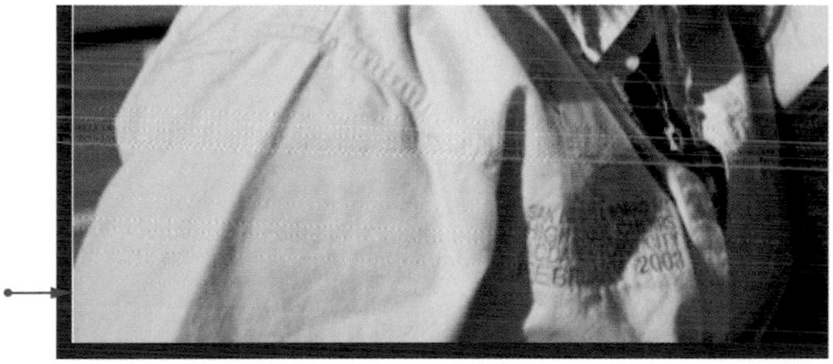

Numerous Statues of Lib

This image was scaled to a size at which it didn't quite fit into its picture box. The hair-thin white line will show on the press sheet. Scan prepress proofs with particular attention to details like this.

Parent's

Parent’s

Many printed projects are flawed by improper punctuation such as typewriter quotes, shown here (top). Proofreaders should check for correct quotation marks and apostrophes (bottom).

What to look for on a press proof

At a press check, plates made from your document are mounted on the press. The press is prepared with the correct inks and paper, and adjustments are made to ensure correct ink density and register. After this process—called *makeready*—is complete, press sheets of your publication are printed and made available for proofing. You, the press operator, and a customer service representative (CSR) then examine the sheets for quality.

At this point, concentrate on corrections that can be made by adjusting the press, such as ink densities or color consistency. It's very expensive to make any other changes to your publication beyond these press adjustments, because it means stopping the press and making new plates. Idle press time is typically charged at $400–$800 per hour plus labor costs; time for web-fed presses is considerably more expensive.

- Is the type sharp? Use a magnifier to look for broken or doubled lines that might indicate the press is slurring or stretching the paper as it's printed.
- Are the colors and type density consistent from one side of the sheet to the other? Remember that ink coverage will vary according to the area of ink printed on the press sheet (number and size of photos and solids).
- Is the color correct? Compare the press sheet to the prepress proof.
- Is the paper or printed surface the one you specified? Bring a sample with you to compare to the press sheet.
- Are page crossovers correct? Fold the press sheet and check the alignment and color match.
- If spot-color inks are used, are they as specified?
- Are there blemishes or mottling of color? Mottling is an indication of an improper balance between moisture (fountain solution) and ink on an offset press. Mottling is often present in correctly printed flexographic work.
- Are all graphic elements present? Compare the press sheet to the prepress proof.
- Are colors in register? Check to make sure all colors line up on the register marks. Under a magnifier, four-color subjects using traditional screening should show a rosette pattern, and no more than a single line of dots of a single color should be visible at the edge of the image.
- Always take a couple of approved press sheets with you for reference.

Color bars

Color bars—those rows of color patches you see on your prepress and press proofs—give proofing and press operators a way to measure and control the press. Although most color bar elements require a densitometer to analyze properly, understanding their purpose can help you evaluate the quality of your printing.

Recognizing color bar elements

Color bars are made up of small patches of colors, tints, and patterns that are grouped in rows across the press sheet. Each element currently used by commercial prepress and press houses is designed for a specific purpose. Common color bar elements can be categorized as follows:

Solid-color patch. The most basic element of a test image is the solid-color patch—one for each of the colors being printed. Solid-color patches are used to measure ink densities, according to the printer's press standards. Printers usually start the press and then *run to the numbers*—reach standard densities—before considering the appearance of color in a printing job.

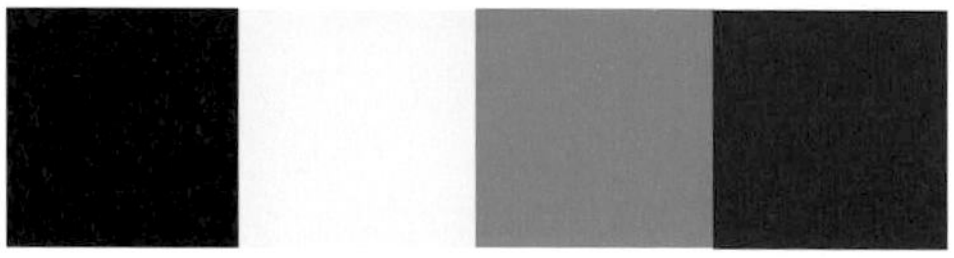

Tint patch. A tint patch is a solid-color patch whose color is less than 100 percent. Most color bars include several patches for each process color set at different tint percentages; the de facto standards in the United States are 25 percent, 50 percent, and 75 percent tints. Tint patches permit the measurement of dot gain because they're created by halftone screens. Dot gain can only be measured in tint areas. Ink lay-down and wet-trapping characteristics (the tack of the ink and its ability to dry correctly on the paper) are also measured with tint patches.

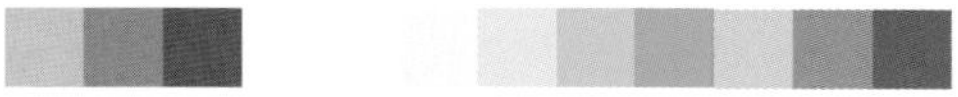

Solid overprint patch. Solid overprint patches show the effects of combining individual solid-color patches. Most color bars include red (magenta and yellow), blue (cyan and magenta), and green (cyan and yellow) solid overprint patches; many also have three- and four-color patches.

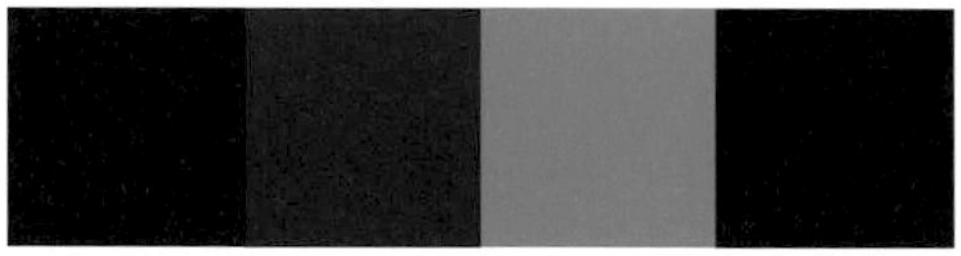

Tint overprint patch. Tint overprint patches combine tint patches of more than one color. These targets are used to monitor the interaction of combinations of standard inks.

Slur gauges. Twisting or kicking of the press sheet by the numerous units in a printing press as the sheet is printed is a problem that is made evident by changes observed in slur gauges in the color bars. These gauges consist of rows of tiny lines that become solid if the sheet twists on the press. One design displays the word *SLUR* when the press sheet encounters this problem. It's usually an indication of trouble with feed and gripper settings on the press.

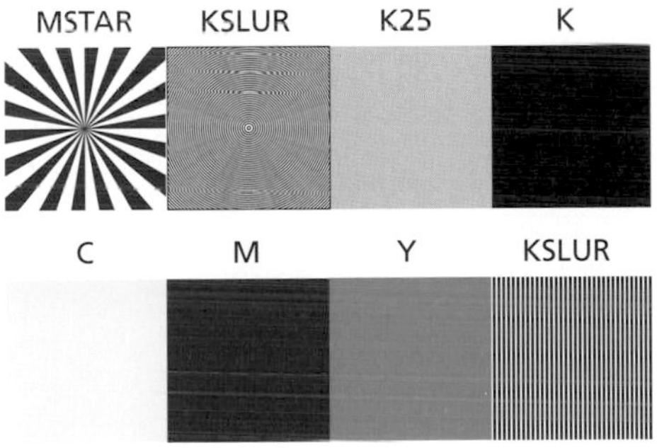

Standard Lighting

If you expect to get predictable results from your color reproduction system, you must consider the lighting where you work and the lighting you use to check proofs. In a professional working environment, you'll find workstations in rooms with no windows; walls painted neutral gray; consistent, color-correct (5,000 Kelvin) lighting; monitors that are calibrated and profiled; and viewing booths with color-correct lighting.

Moderately priced color viewing booths are available for graphic design studios. These booths provide correct-color lighting and thus give you an opportunity to view your proofs and printed samples in industry-standard lighting conditions.

Archiving Your Work

To be useful in the future as a source of images and text, your document should be archived in a format that is likely to remain in widespread use for a long time. Be cautious when you're archiving your document in proprietary formats or in formats specific to an application: the file format, or the application used to create it, may become obsolete.

Adobe is working to develop industry standard file formats that will remain useful for many years. The company's *Digital Negative* format, designed for digital photographers, is gaining momentum as a standard for the storage of raw photo files, ensuring that those files will be legible to computers in the decades to come.

Portable Document Format (PDF) provides a way to store publications in a format that can be viewed and printed with 100 percent fidelity. Archived PDF files can be opened, printed, and exchanged in any of the common environments, including Macintosh, Windows, and Unix. Large libraries of PDF files can be indexed and searched. The PDF format should be legible for many generations of computers.

It's a great idea to make a high-resolution (press quality) PDF of your final document to save as a reference of what went to press *in addition to the original document elements.* This archive PDF can also be used to make an electronic version of your document.

Print production is an expertise that most designers don't take seriously. Good production techniques will make or break the design.

—Mary K. Baumann, Hopkins/Baumann, New York, NY

Case Study: Black & White Design

The Black & White Design client list reads like a Who's Who of Silicon Valley, with companies such as Adobe Systems, Apple Computer, Cisco Systems, Hewlett-Packard, Seagate, Sun, and Symantec. But the Campbell, California-based design firm's work takes it far beyond high-tech, designing logos and collateral materials for wineries, non-profit organizations, even a farming company.

For logo design, the company's designers always use Adobe Illustrator, sometimes in combination with Adobe Photoshop. For multi-page composition, the firm recently made the shift to InDesign and the Adobe Creative Suite.

Black & White Design works with trusted suppliers to produce the work they send to print, and the relationships are long-term and mutually respectful. "When we ask for estimates, we speak 'printer language,'" said founder Nicki Riedel. "We structure our requests for estimates the way they work, and then we provide correctly prepared files and comprehensive proofs for production that reflect the original direction. The printers know they can count on us to be thorough, and that enables success with each project. We have extremely high standards, and our suppliers make sure we achieve them."

In many cases, Riedel thinks that the design firm should work the color until it is what the designer envisioned, "I prefer that we, as designers, do the color correction and proofing. In those cases, we can tell the printer that all the high-resolution images have been placed and that the file is ready to print. For some very large files or very complex photo manipulation, we use a color house."

When working with illustrators and photographers, Riedel says, "Choose an artist who has the right style for the project. Know what you want, and provide good direction. For illustration, provide rough sketches, if possible, and have them initially produce two for approval. I suggest choosing the easiest and the most difficult—or the smallest and largest—first to test the water and provide an opportunity for the art director to make changes before much work is done."

Once production has begun, the entire project team stays close to its projects—start to finish. They make their own proofs on either the Epson Stylus Pro 10600 ink-jet printer, the Canon Color Laser 1120, or the Hewlett-Packard Color Laserjet 5500. Each has its own advantages. The designers know what they are looking for and choose the printer that will produce their work best.

"We make our own proofs and have learned that we can show them to customers and print suppliers to get the results we expect," says Riedel. Many times her firm uses the same technology they are promoting to design the printing. "It has to look great, and we work hard to ensure complete success."

SILVERADO
FARMING COMPANY

ANGEL INVESTORS

Aspect commuter Connection

Centraal RN

Art Docents of Los Gatos

Logos designed by Black & White Design show the diversity of their work. Striking high-tech or charming old-world symbols are designed according to the needs of the clients.

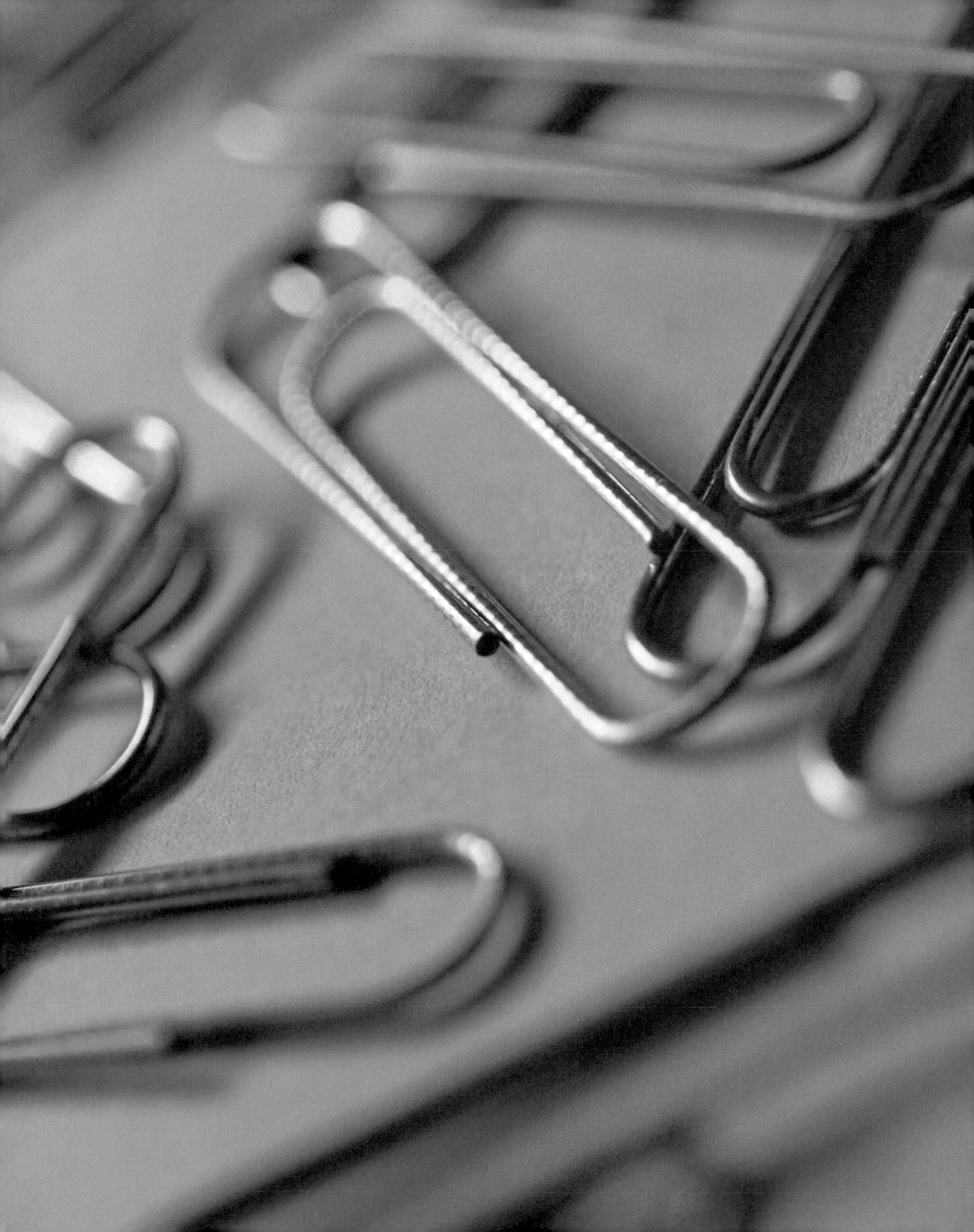

4 Project Management Guidelines

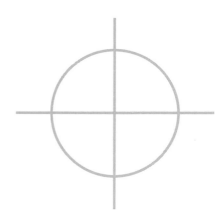

Project Management Guidelines

Every commercial printing job requires that you consider numerous variables ranging from what your budget and schedule allow to the paper stock and printing process. The earlier you think about these factors, the more control you'll have over the quality, cost, and schedule of your project.

Preparing a publication for commercial printing takes careful thought: Commercial printing processes have inherent limitations, and it's possible to create publications that are difficult to print. By thinking of your design and production cycles as steps in a larger process, you can make choices that will allow you to achieve the best printed results.

In addition to choosing a commercial printer, you may need to select a separate prepress service. One-stop shopping can prevent misunderstandings and improve quality control. Prepress work can include scanning, color trapping, imposition, and platemaking. Several types of vendors provide these services: prepress houses, color trade shops, and color-capable service bureaus, as well as most commercial printers. Shop for vendors who are willing to answer your printing questions, provide technical support, and help you to achieve your printing objectives.

The Publishing Process

Successfully completing a printed publication requires several steps, including planning and organization, design and content development, and prepress tasks that prepare your electronic files to be reproduced with ink on paper.

Making informed decisions in the planning stages builds a solid foundation for your project. When you have questions about your project, seek advice from your vendors. Keep track of decisions you make: who is responsible for the completion and quality of each task, when each phase must be completed, and what requirements must be met for the final output.

1. Define project and quality requirements

Before you start to work, define the requirements for the publication, including your budget, the schedule, and the final quality you want.

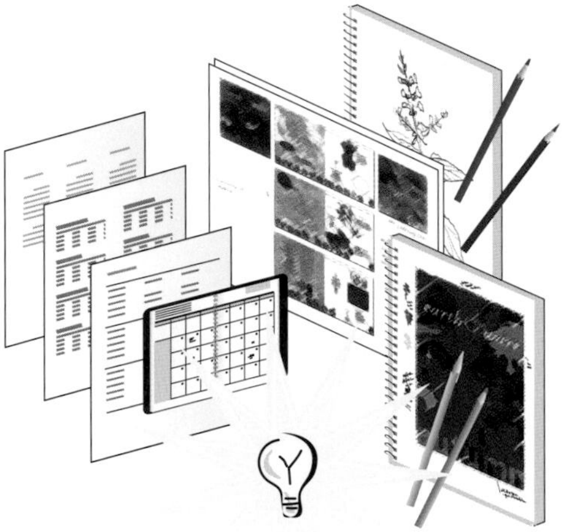

2. Choose prepress tasks

Determine which prepress tasks you'll do, based on your available resources and the final schedule. Specialized tasks such as trapping and imposition will probably be part of the work done by the prepress firm or the printer.

3. Select and consult your vendors

Evaluate commercial printers and prepress service providers based on the requirements of your project and the services you require. Review samples of their work, and choose vendors who can provide the quality you demand. Visit the sites of potential vendors if possible. Select a commercial printer early in the process so they can assist you in planning your project.

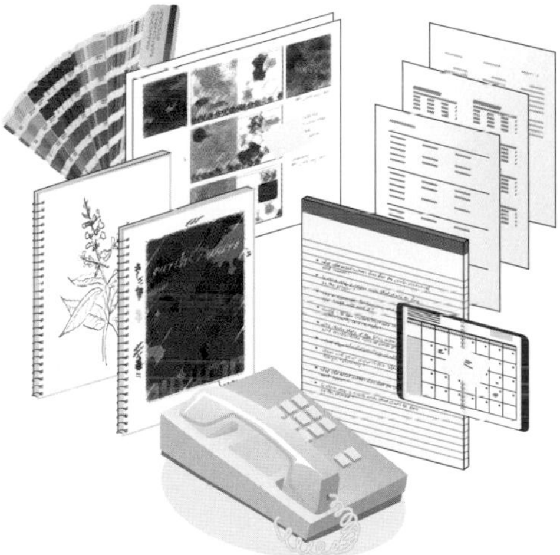

4. Create your publication

Define the number of colors you'll use, including process and spot colors (or both). Select the paper on which your job will print, and make sure the printer you've selected agrees that the paper is a good choice. Some papers have better printing characteristics than others; you should be sure yours doesn't create a press problem.

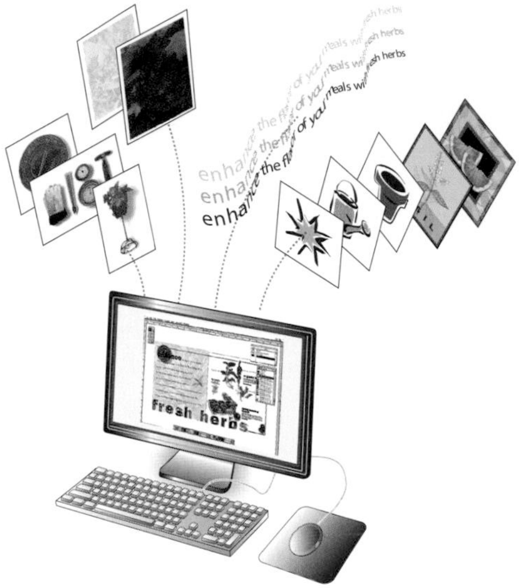

Assemble the text and the vector, raster, and line art for your publication. Review the design to determine how the page elements interact and overlap. Determine, by communication with your printer, who will be responsible for the conversion of color in images. Ask the printer to provide an ICC color profile if possible. Discuss any printing issues with your printer as your design evolves.

5. Check the desktop proofs

Print proof copies of your publication on a black-and-white or color PostScript desktop printer. Consult your printer about the recommended proofing methods to check color quality and to ensure against production problems.

6. Hand off your files

Through communication with your prepress provider, determine what type of files to prepare. Run a preflight check on your document; then, package your files and prepare the final desktop proofs, a report listing details about your document, and any additional files. Coordinate with the customer service representative at the printing plant or service bureau, and turn over the files to them on the appropriate medium.

7. Check the final proofs, and authorize printing

Examine the proof provided by your printer for quality and correctness. Check proofs for correct trapping, and for smooth and consistent tints. If appropriate, meet with your printer to review press proofs for final color quality. After you approve the press proof, the publication will be printed and assembled.

8. Archive your publication

After your publication has been printed, you need to store all your files in a consistent manner so that you can quickly find and update them if needed. Decide what type of storage media you'll use, and develop a file-naming system that lets you search for all files needed to revise or reprint your publication.

And, remember that all great designers "steal" from their previous works. Artwork prepared for one project can easily be reused on similar projects, thus saving you time and money. Within the terms of use agreed on between your firm and photographers, illustrators, and writers, some material from one publication can easily find its way into other projects. A good archiving system allows for the quick access to files, illustrations, and artwork used in earlier projects.

disc
Recordable

Money Matters

Every print project requires you to balance costs, schedule, and quality. When you're preparing a budget, estimate fixed and variable costs. Fixed costs don't vary depending on how many copies of the job you print. These costs include payment for designing, writing, editing, photography, and print preparation. Variable costs—those costs that vary depending on how many copies you print—include press time, paper, and binding.

Estimate the resources and skills of the workgroup assigned to the project. If you have the skills and equipment to do some of the prepress work in house, it can be cheaper than having the work done by an outside contractor.

Avoid last-minute changes. Modifications made late in the project cycle can result in missed press dates, additional charges from the printer, and delays in binding and delivery. As a general rule, the closer changes are made to the press date, the more costly they are.

If you and your service provider understand each other's requirements, you can both take steps to stay on-budget while ensuring the project's success.

Reviewing Your Requirements

Both the cost and the impact of your publication are greatly affected by the printing process. The cost can also be affected by your schedule—a rush job is more costly than a job the printer can run on a normal schedule. Asking yourself the following questions may help you arrive at requirements appropriate to your project:

- **Audience:** How do you need to influence your audience? Does the printed piece have to distinguish itself visually from similar pieces? Does it have to get the attention of an audience to inform them, or is the audience anticipating the information in the piece? Must the piece appeal visually to design-conscious buyers?
- **Length of time on the market:** Is this a publication that announces a one-time-only offer (like a sale flyer), or will it be used over and over again (like a cookbook)?
- **Image issues:** Is visual detail important to the message? Illustrations in a history textbook may not be color-critical, but the detail must be clear for the image to be informative. Flesh tones should always look human and healthy. Images for a clothing catalog require clear detail, especially for fine prints and textures.
- **Color matching:** Will people make critical decisions based on the color in the piece? Clothing catalogs usually require an exact match to the actual clothing. If the color is wrong, customers may be dissatisfied with the clothing they receive. In other cases, it's more important for colors to be balanced; food images in grocery ads or cookbooks require a pleasing photograph but not necessarily a color match.

Sample requirements

Newsletters The newsletter is printed with one color of ink (usually black), photographs are recognizable but may lose some detail from the original, and the paper stock is a standard type that's always on hand. The piece is designed to be read and discarded. Timeliness is the most important factor with newsletters.

Direct-mail catalog The catalog is printed using paper that's regularly kept in stock by the printer. The standard size makes it cheaper to bind and finish. The catalog includes crisp black-and-white photographs and color photographs with good detail. Color accuracy is important but not critical, because buying decisions aren't usually based on the represented color. Color register must be accurate. The publication will be replaced in several months.

Fine clothing catalog This catalog uses premium papers and inks. Color in the photographs is required to match the actual clothing. Press register must be very accurate, and all the artwork must be trapped perfectly. Although the expected life of the publication is short, a high-quality publication helps persuade the customer to buy.

Corporate annual report In an annual report, the image of the company is conveyed by the quality of design, printing, and appearance of the publication. Color, although less critical than in a clothing catalog, is accurate; and black-and-white photographs are very sharp. The product can have no discernible flaws.

Who Does What?

One of the decisions you must make regarding a project is how much of the prepress work you'll do yourself. With the expanding range of electronic publishing tools, you may be tempted to do many of the tasks yourself. But tasks that can be done on the desktop require skill, time, and equipment you may not have or want to acquire.

At the final stage, you must make a critical decision about the format in which you hand off your files. Your prepress provider may prefer that you turn over files in their native format (using *Package* or *Collect for Output*) and let the vendor convert them to PostScript for imaging onto plates. In that case, you hand over files in the formats appropriate to your page-layout, illustration, or image-editing programs, and the vendor converts them. Or your prepress vendor may recommend that you convert your document to Adobe PDF format, using settings recommended by the prepress firm.

The following is intended to help weigh the trade-offs in choosing prepress tasks.

Scanning, digital camera images, and color correction

Most original photos originate as digital camera images. If you work with a professional photographer, you can ask the photographer to make any color corrections needed prior to transferring the images to you, or you can make color corrections yourself on a calibrated computer display.

If you're working with film or photographic prints, you can scan the images yourself using a flatbed or film scanner, or you can choose to have your prepress vendor do the scanning for you.

Although they're becoming rare, some prepress service providers use a drum scanner that delivers superb image quality. Drum-scanning is costly, but you may need the greater resolution that it provides. Along with the high-resolution files, low-resolution versions (called OPI files) can also be provided to speed up design and proofing.

Doing your own image editing and color correction can be time consuming, but you have complete control over the appearance of the final image. Most graphic designers enjoy the creative options that are provided by having the full-resolution images at their disposal along with the many powerful tools available in Adobe Photoshop to enhance those images.

Trapping

It's likely that several of the desktop tools you're already using—such as illustration, image-editing, and page-layout programs—can apply trapping automatically or semi-automatically. For example, Adobe Illustrator lets you trap color artwork before it's imported into a page-layout application.

Although doing so may seem like a good idea, it's seldom appreciated by the prepress vendor, because this sort of trapping isn't as sophisticated as that available on their equipment. In addition, artwork that's trapped manually often prevents the automated trapping functions in prepress from doing their job. When generating halftone screens, they already know how much to allow for dot gain.

Color mode conversion

You can convert your document from its native color to the process color necessary for printing, after communication with your prepress vendor; or the prepress vendor can perform the conversion as part of the preparation they do in advance of printing.

As long as you and your prepress supplier agree on the method and the ICC profiles applied, the conversion of color is a reasonably easy step that can save you some time (and perhaps a bit of cost) if you do it yourself. However, some prepress specialists prefer that you hand your files over for production in native mode (some images in RGB color, for example) and then leave the conversion to them.

Converting files to Adobe PDF

Many commercial printers have adopted a workflow that uses full-resolution Adobe PDF files as source material for printing. If you and your printer have agreed that this will be the workflow for your project, be sure to obtain the proper settings files (or your printer's recommendation of standard settings) from the printer before making your own PDF files.

PDF workflows are significantly simpler than those in which all the contributing files are provided in native format. There is just one document, all fonts are embedded in that document, and all the illustrations and images are included.

The disadvantage can be that corrections—even simple typographic corrections—are often impossible to make in the PDF file. Making modifications requires you to generate a new master document to provide for production.

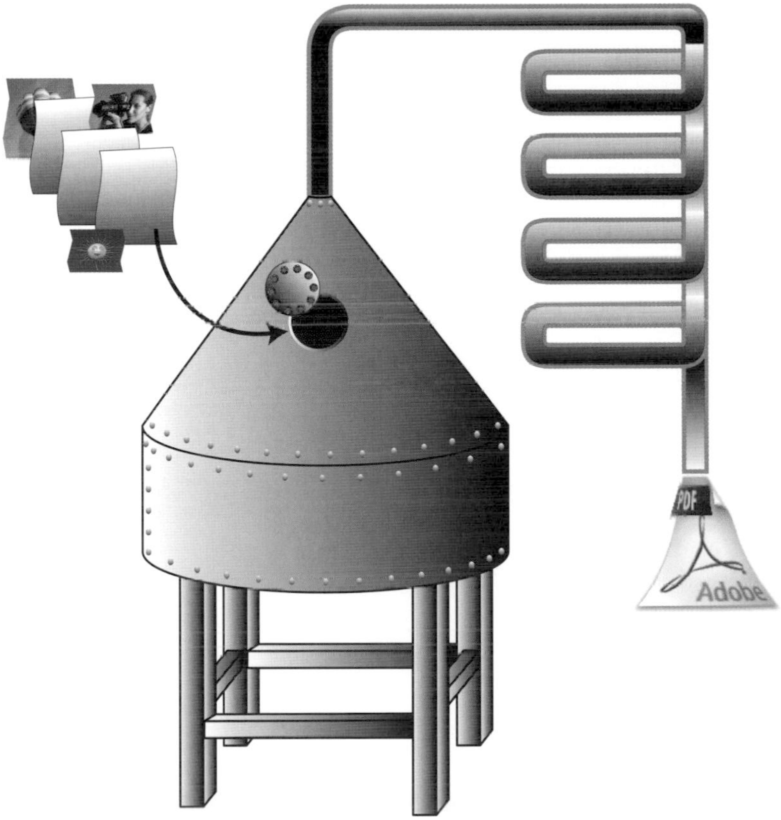

Case Study: Designer Rob Corder

Designers always need to push the limits of what is possible," says artist and designer Rob Corder, of the interior design firm Ann Getty and Associates (www.anngetty.com), based in San Francisco. "No client or printer appreciates the status quo. There would be a great lack of delight, grace, or wonderment in life without artists pushing beyond what is known."

This beautiful die-cut invitation (opposite page), designed by Corder, is an excellent example of pushing the limits of printing. The complex die-cut design is styled after the motif from a Georgian chair in Getty's line of fine furniture. Corder used Adobe Illustrator to design the invitation and its die-cutting pattern. "I love using layers in Illustrator. I can't image doing this any other way," he said.

The invitation was printed by Color Copy Printing/The Lahlouh Group, of Burlingame, California. "Color Copy Printing recommended we laser-cut this project, due to the intricate pattern and the need to keep it in perfect alignment. It was my first experience with laser cutting, and it produced a wonderful result. If the paper remains white, laser cutting leaves a burn mark along the edges of the pattern. I flooded the die-cut area with red ink, so that edge effect is not apparent."

Corder says he prefers working with prepress firms that are on the same site as the printer so there's closer communication and a greater sense of shared responsibility. "I prefer to use printers who have done comparable quality work to what I'm expecting. And I rarely use a print broker, since the lifeline of communication is broken between the designer and the printer."

And printer loyalty is key for this designer. "I prefer going back to the same providers. There's an established dialog, and like any great partnership, they know your sense of style and shared standard of excellence."

How does he ensure that his intended colors comes come through on the final product? "The best way to ensure you get exact colors is to get an ink draw-down. It stretches out the production time but gives you peace of mind that a critical piece is going to be spot-on."

On the age-old balance of quality and price, Corder says, "When you start a project by specifying great paper, it sets the bar at certain height and guarantees a standard of quality in your work. I really appreciate quality over price. I find it uncommon to see inferior printed pieces on a luxurious paper. Most great projects start with the best materials."

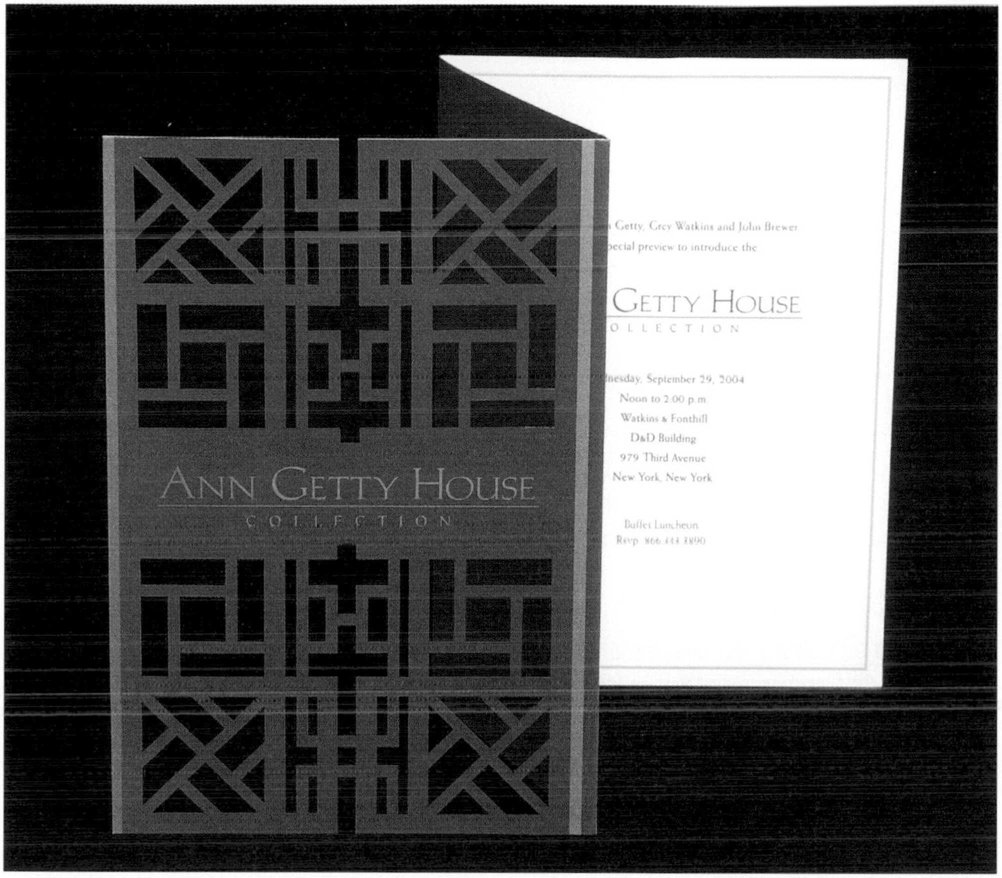

Ann Getty House
Collection
Getty, Grey Watkins and John Brewer
preview to introduce the
Getty House
September 29, 2004
Noon to 2:00 p.m.
Watkins & Fonthill
D&D Building
979 Third Avenue
New York, New York
Buffet Luncheon

Selecting Vendors

Word of mouth is the best way to find a good printing firm. Ask around, and you'll learn quickly about local printers and their work.

Or you can examine printed material that is similar to your project and find out who printed it. Decide whether you want to work with a commercial printer that does the prepress work in house, or whether you prefer to have prepress work done at a different location. Obtaining prepress services from a commercial printer allows you to communicate with just one vendor and manage only one relationship. If you choose to work with several vendors, make sure they understand each other's requirements and are comfortable working with each other.

Questions to ask about prepress services

- What proofing options are available, and how many proofing cycles are permitted? Is the recommended proofing option reflective of the final output?
- What file formats do they accept? From which platforms?
- Do they offer scanning? Do they offer—and accept—OPI files?
- Do they use trapping software?
- Do they support color management using ICC profiles? Can they provide an ICC profile for the presses that will print your job?

Questions to ask about printing

- Are both sheet-fed and web-fed presses available? The former are fed individual sheets of paper, print more slowly, and tend to be used for most commercial jobs. The latter are fed from a continuous roll, print faster (tens of thousands of impressions per hour), and are used for very long runs. The nature of your job determines which is preferable.
- How many colors can be printed in one press run? A two-color press requires two press runs to print process color. You'll be able to cut costs—and get a better printing job—by shopping for a commercial printer with a four-color press.
- Do they provide bindery and finishing services in house? Will they be able to complete your project on time? Do they have responsive customer service representatives?

Careful planning is the best defense against unexpected problems. Test everything early in production—fonts, scanned art, EPS graphics, etc. —when mistakes are cheaper and easier to fix. Make a thorough checklist and follow it religiously.

—Eric and Jan Martí, Command Z, Palo Alto, CA

Decisions Involving Your Printer

Once you've made a choice, discuss the specifics of the project with your printer. You may wish to inquire about the following:

- Color settings to use, ICC profiles to set for proofing, and color mode conversion
- Any trap specifications your job should have
- Any other recommended settings or processes to use

The printer may have recommendations related to your design and choice of color. Having the right paper stock, coating, and ink types is important to the quality of your final publication, and the availability of critical materials can affect scheduling. You may wish to bring up some of the following topics:

- Your project schedule and budget
- The dimensions of your publication and how many copies you plan to print
- The colors you plan to specify
- Decisions about finishing and binding
- Your use of bleeds and crossovers
- The graphics in your publication

Your printer may have recommendations concerning materials, bindings, or special inks and may be able to point out ways to save money by making minor changes in your publication. Discussing the project gives the printer a chance to notice if particular inks and grades of paper need to be ordered in advance.

File Handoff Checklist

Minimize surprises and surcharges from your prepress vendor by using the following checklist when preparing your files for handoff.

Create a logical filename. Many documents arrive for production named "brochure" or "document 1." Using machine-generated names for your document is unwise, because your "document 1" can be confused with another "document 1." Instead, give your document a name like "Cabinet Booklet" or "Valves Brochure" so that the name is a good identifier.

Eliminate all unnecessary elements. Delete all extraneous colors, patterns, and other elements from the file, including those that may be invisible or behind other elements or layers.

Use the correct format. Make sure all files are in the correct format. Consult your prepress vendor for the best file format to use.

Make spot color names consistent. If you use the same spot color several times in one document, be consistent in specifying each object's color. If you want the vendor to convert certain spot colors to process colors, indicate where you want that done.

Provide a desktop proof. Print your files first on a PostScript laser printer. Send these laser prints with your files, so the prepress vendor can check against them, making sure the prints are identical to the files in every respect: size (unless you've scaled your proof), content, placement, bleeds, crops, traps, and so forth.

Package all graphics and document files. Using your page-layout application, choose the *Package* or *Collect for Output* function to copy all the graphics and fonts required for your project.

Provide contact information. In a work order or cover letter (or in the *Instructions* file created by Adobe InDesign), list your name, company name, and phone numbers, including after-hours numbers. Include your document specifications (quantity, page size, colors, and so on), because this information will travel with the document and become part of the job ticket generated by the printer when your job goes into production.

CE

Index

D

E

F

G

M

N

O

P

Q

R

S

About the Author

Brian P. Lawler started his first printing company at age 11, worked his way through high school as a printer, and graduated with a Bachelor's degree in Graphic Communication from California Polytechnic State University, in San Luis Obispo, CA.

He launched a design, typography, and prepress business in San Luis Obispo, which he ran for 18 years before leaving the company to become an industry consultant. He has lectured on color management and prepress for companies including Apple, Adobe, Hewlett-Packard, and Eastman Kodak, and has worked as a printing consultant for more than a decade.

He is now an instructor at Cal Poly University, teaching courses in graphic communication, digital typography, prepress, and color management. A contributor to CreativePro.com and InDesign Magazine, Brian has also authored several books, including *The Complete Guide to Trapping.*

presentationzen
The Digital Photography Book
Scott Kelby
The Non-Designer's Design Book
Third Edition
Robin Williams
ADOBE ILLUSTRATOR CS4
CLASSROOM IN A BOOK
DREAMWEAVER CS4
VISUAL QUICKSTART GUIDE
ADOBE FIREWORKS CS4 HOW-TOS
100 ESSENTIAL TECHNIQUES
designing with web standards second edition zeldman
THE BRAND GAP MARTY NEUMEIER
designing the moment web interface design concepts in action
HTML, XHTML & CSS
SIXTH EDITION
VISUAL QUICKSTART GUIDE
SECOND EDITION
DON'T MAKE ME THINK!
WEB USABILITY
KRUG
ADOBE DREAMWEAVER CS4
CLASSROOM IN A BOOK
BREAKING OUT OF THE WEB BROWSER
WITH ADOBE AIR
Designing Web Usability
Jakob Nielsen
CLICKS
MCNALLY
ADOBE INDESIGN CS4
CLASSROOM IN A BOOK
PHOTOSHOP CS4
VISUAL QUICKSTART GUIDE
ADOBE FLASH CS4 PROFESSIONAL
CLASSROOM IN A BOOK